CAN I HAVE MY BALLS BACK PLEASE?

DOTUN ADEBAYO

WITH ILLUSTRATIONS BY DANIEL FRANCIS

The
X
Press

Published by The X Press
PO Box 25694, London N17 6P7
Tel: 020 8801 2100
Fax: 020 8885 1322
Email: vibes@xpress.co.uk
Web site: www. xpress.co.uk

Printed by Omnia Books Limited, Glasgow

Distributed in US by INBOOK, 1436 West Randolph Street, Chicago, Illinois 60607,
USA Orders 1-800 626 4330 Fax orders 1-800 334 3892

Distributed in UK by Turnaround Distribution, Unit 3, Olympia Trading Estate,
Coburg Road, London N22 6TZ
Tel: 0181 829 3000
Fax: 0181 881 5088

ISBN 1-874509-87-5

Cover photo by David Corio

THE MALE EUNUCH

I'd like to take this opportunity to make an emotional appeal to y'all (women) on behalf of us all (men):

CAN WE HAVE OUR BALLS BACK, PLEASE?

Women are always complaining about how hard it is to find a real man nowadays. Is it any wonder, when fellas have been gradually castrated over the last thirty years since the publication of Germaine Greer's feminist bible The Female Eunuch.

Back in the days when men were young, free and single enough to kick ass and wreck a poom-poom or two, we had balls. Not ping-pong size, but great big bouncy, juicy, brightly-coloured balls with knobs on.

We spent many a happy hour hanging on to them, comparing shapes and sizes to the tune of Hitler Has Only Got One Ball, reassured in the knowledge that at least we had a matching pair (little knowing that Hitler would have the last laugh).

New Millennium Man has lost his balls. Under manners, he no longer flaunts his testicles in front of all and sundry but spends his life listening to the devil in his right ear advising him of the consequences of infidelity, when the devil in his left ear done already told him that he can get away with it scot free.

So while we've lost our balls, guess who's got them?

Why is it, that the moment you settle down with a woman the first thing she goes for is your gonads?

I remember years back, seeing this Woody Allen film where, in a future world, men were the slaves of the ruling female population. Men had been turned into virtual eunuchs and women ruled with a rod of iron. The film was of course a comedy and it had me in stitches. Years on, the BBC are afraid to show the film for fear that men in their thousands will throws themselves off high-rise buildings with the realisation that this distant world ain't so far away.

Men (black men and white men in particular) are not happy. Unhappy men do not make good partners/fathers/lovers/drinking companions/rugby players.

Something terrible is happening to us guys . We are not being allowed to do what we do best — be guys. Suddenly we're public enemy number one and women are queuing up to cut our balls off. Am I being paranoid, or is it that woman who keeps following me everywhere waving her scalpel that is? Get a group of women together for an evening drinks session, and I swear by the end of the evening you can hear them chanting "Burn him, burn him!"

Only two weeks ago my spar asked a woman at a club for her digits and she looked at him with total disdain and snarled, "I don't date men!" He tried to show common ground by saying, "What a coincidence, nor do I."

While men are wondering what's going on, women are packing out the 'Untap the Beast Within' spiritual assertiveness training workshops, where they are taught how to remove a man's testicles at twenty yards

Women don't need assertive training, it's men that should be enrolling. So many women I know these days seem to have testicles bigger than mine and the bollocks to go with them.

It is time to say enough is enough, or, in other words, please can we have our balls back, ladies? And our deep throats, too, because I don't know how much more I can take of this modern man business.

MY BALLS AND HOW I LOST THEM

New Man. New Age Bloke. Renaissance Man. 21st Century Guy... It's all bollocks! 'Cause when you check it out, there are only two kinds of men in the world: Tits Men and Arse Men.

"So, which one are you?" Sweetie asked me.

"Ah...uhm....erm..."

If you truly want honesty, ladies, don't ask guys questions you don't really want the answer to.

I muttered something about how I was attracted to a woman's mind, her personality, etc etc.

Yeah. Right. Bollocks.

Sweetie didn't fall for it, either.

"Come on, put yourself on the line," she insisted, "are you a Tits Man or an Arse Man?"

I tried to laugh it off but finally succumbed to a compromise. "I swing both ways..."

Now, if she was a man, I wouldn't have to lie. I would have told her straight. 'Cause a man would know exactly what it means to be a Tits Man.

No matter what he may say in public, in private when a Tits Man says he finds a woman attractive, he means he loves the size of her chest. It's not necessarily the bigger the better. Sometimes less is more, especially if the nipples have got you in their sight. Few things get a man going like the 'friendly fire' from a rock-hard nipple.

As a general rule, the more intriguing the breasts the easier it is to hypnotise the Tits Man. Indeed, I spent my early teens being mesmerised by women's chests. It was easier to be a Tits Man then, but as I grew taller I could hardly hold a conversation with a woman without being caught out with my gaze down.

No wonder Tits Men tend to be short.

Arse Men, however, don't have the same problem.

Arse Men are the big batty girls' secret admirers. The scores of male eyes that follow that jelly booty wherever it goes. And you don't have to do it on the sly, either (unless women suddenly develop eyes on the back of their heads). No need to sneak glimpses. Take your time. Kick back, relax, take in two eyefuls. Study, evaluate, admire, get your juices stirring.

My juices stir, 2-3000 times a day. That's south

London for you!

Now, a hardcore Tits Man can never understand an Arse Man. The Tits Man gets turned on by the body parts that he ain't got — breasts that are bigger than his. Torpedoes which scream, 'Hey fellas, look at us!' And that's it. "Instead of all those subliminal, arty ads in the press and telly why can't advertisers just use large-breasted women to flog their goods?" the Tits Man often wonders.

Try as hard as he may, the Tits Man just doesn't get turned on by a backside.

An Arse Man, on the other hand, is a real connoisseur. He can appreciate good tits but won't commit himself until he's seen the behind. He'll compose an ode to it and discuss it philosophically. He'll burn down his house, leave his wife and sell his kids for a good arse, long before introducing himself to the bloke it belongs to...

Bootys being genderless, it is vital to not only check out the shape or size but also the way it's carried. That's what makes men grin and wink at each other saying, "Look at the batty on dat!"

That's what made me scream, "I'D LIKE A PIECE AH DAT!" and nearly made my eyes pop out when (KABAAM!) I screeched to a halt on that hot, sunny day in the month of May to allow Miss Bootyfabulous to juggle her backside across the Balls Pond Road. I was staring so hard I caused a multi-car pile-up and didn't even know it.

"So you'd really like a piece of that?" said the little voice in my left ear.

"Sure bloody. That booty is outta this world, it can sit on my face any time! I gotta find out what time those legs open! I wanna wrap them around my head and bang her till I'm blue."

"So you'd really, *really* like a piece of that?" said that voice in my ear again.

"If I'm lyin', I'm flyin'. I love that butt so much I'd like to wear it as a hat!"

You see, a butt this good can trick your mind into thinking that you're sitting in your car alone, when in reality your woman's in the front passenger seat with a testicle garotte, pretending to be the little voice of your conscience.

Imagine my surprise when my balls exploded with pain.

HEY!

LOST YOUR BALLS?

We can replace them!!

BEFORE

AFTER

Full size or miniatures. Mounting Service and Ribbons. S.A.E. for replacement list to Mr Toad, Toad hall, P.O. Box 110CK5, Goolies-Under-Cock, UK FU2.

HOW TO SPOT A MAN WHO HAS LOST HIS BALLS

1. He calls his woman. ALWAYS.

2. He DOESN'T nickname his cock.

3. He NEVER plays with himself, nor tells everyone about it.

4. He hasn't had more women than showers.

5. People always think he has no penis.

6. He never goes after his woman's best friend.

7. If he doesn't get laid whenever he wants, his balls don't shrivel.

8. He has feelings.

9. He believes the basic fundamental rule of sex is quality NOT quantity.

10. He is light on his feet.

WHO WOULD YOU LIKE TO SLEEP WITH?

In secondary school, I dated a girl with huge tits, but there was no passion. So at university I dated a passionate girl, but she was too emotional. She cried all the time. So I dated a girl with some stability. She was very stable, but she was boring. She never got excited about anything. So I decided I needed a girl with some excitement. I found an exciting girl, but I couldn't keep up with her. She rushed from one thing to another, never settling on anything. So I dated a girl with ambition and married her. She was so ambitious, she divorced me and took everything I owned. Now all I want is a girl with huge tits.

Ladies, nothing in the world can keep your man faithful if his penis is his best chance of becoming a member of MENSA. You can cook for him and wash for him and iron all his clothes. You can lose weight, get trim, buy sexy new clothes and go down on him, but as sure as the sun will shine, he'll still go out and find someone else to swallow it (sometimes, anyone will do).

You see, from the moment his friends start complimenting him on how 'criss' his woman looks, my man is already thinking that if he can pull one pretty hot and tempting gal, he can pull another. Remember, it's the male ego we're dealing with here.

I've known a woman who sold her home and spent the profit on a wotless partner, in the vain hope that she might buy exclusive rights to his long donkey dickey. It was like she was paying him to stick around (excuse the metaphor).

She lied and cried many times for him and even agreed to be tied up for him! And all because he assured her that he had been cured of his need to dip his wick in every available hole. Like hell he had been cured! The moment my man was outta jail, he followed his dick on a world tour.

Please ladies, check your man's IQ both above and below the belt. If his cock is bigger than his IQ, you know he's never going to remain faithful.

I know you won't accept what I'm saying. Because since the beginning of time women have been believing that they can turn any man round. Some women even claim that what they've got is so sweet

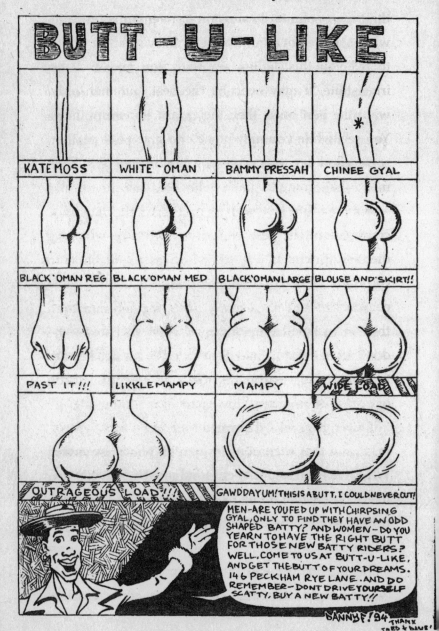

their man voluntarily slips on a silver penis restraint when they're not around to keep an eye on him. I hate to tell you this, ladies, sex with you may well be irresistible, it may even be the best, but men only want the best once, then they want something new. You see, while you may be able to give your partner some good sex, you can't give him no *new* sex. That means he's going to go elsewhere to find it.

You see, life for most men is like one big pussy competition. The guy who scores the most when he dies is the winner. I know, some guys will try and convince you that they're not even in the competition. That's because they're so far behind they've resigned themselves with the fact that they don't have a chance of winning. But they don't want to come last, either. So they 'jump on' every opportunity to increase their average. You get me?

Other guys will claim that they are a new type of man, and that they don't wanna be playas no more. Why, I've even said that out loud myself, while in my heart I knew that if I had a chance to go for the world title I would. Because every man wants to be a winner, baby.

Besides, at the end of the day, you sleep with a woman night after night and, pretty soon, passion dies its natural death.

I told Sweetie as much: "Man cannot live by bread alone."

Ask even the least intelligent penis to interpret this and you'll find it loosely translated as: 'Same old sex every day drives willy silly and eventually it will wither and die'.

So, ladies, you're going to have to keep that love light burning bright to compete. You're going to need vibrating beds, water beds, jacuzzis, porno videos, a variety of sex toys and a video camera in your mirrored bedrooms. And if that fails, you need to turn to your man and ask him straight:

WHO WOULD YOU LIKE TO SLEEP WITH, DEAR?

If I posed the above question to my spar Tony I can bet the answer would be, 'everyone'. Tony's like that. He doesn't have any concept of the meaning of the word 'discernment'. 'Two tits, a hole and a heartbeat' is all that it takes for our Tone. It's so refreshing to meet a person in this 'want, want want' society who is so easily pleased.

For the rest of us, discernment and selection are a normal part of male/female interaction and attraction. We are all aware of the role race plays in attraction because generally we tend to be more attracted to those of our own race. But what role does nationality play when it comes to who we fancy?

If you got a group of Nigerians, Jamaicans or Bajans together, would the different groups have different views on who was and wasn't sexy? A recent survey commissioned by condom makers Durex gives some clues.

'Let's Talk About Sex' was conducted with 10,000 sexually active adults aged between 16 to 45 years old in fourteen different countries. One of the questions asked was 'Which famous person would you most want to go to bed with?' The differences in national tastes were extremely varied. For example, in Britain, Naomi Campbell received the smallest number of thumbs up. Only 6% of British males wanted to bonk her. In contrast 36% of Italian stallions were rearing to get their leg over her. Is it just that Brits don't like Naomi or are they turned off by black women? We don't know.

When it came to the ladies, 26% of English roses said they wouldn't mind being pricked by Denzel Washington. However, this is small when compared with 37% of Australians or 41% of American women. My advise to any black guys trying to pull in Moscow is, forget it, geezer, too much like hard work. Only 3%

of Russian gals said they would like to see Denzel in their duvet.

So, who would the average British male most like to shag? I was surprised myself, but apparently it was GI Jane herself, Demi Moore. 34% of British males said they would stand to attention if Demi walked across their parade ground. No disrespect to Demi, but hers is one booty which really don't get my meat throbbing. The average guy like myself would choose Naomi and her mum Valerie, Charmaine Sinclair and Lil' Kim. All together, and at the same time. Then for the main course I'd have.....

Now, the typical British woman's choice of Brad Pitt as their No.1 shagging partner was more predictable. 47% said that they'd like to play at being a miner for the night (they'd like to go down pitt).

Sometimes, though, too much choice can be a bad thing. If you're a half presentable black man looking for a relationship, the choice of female partners available has never been greater. Go to most social functions, and if you're a man you will have the upper hand. Nine out of ten times, women will outnumber the guys by a considerable margin. I can't in recent memory recall a time when I went somewhere and the ladies didn't vastly outnumber

Sometimes we men have too many choices

the men. When it comes to thirtysomethings, the ratio imbalance becomes even greater.

As a black man the options don't just stop at black women. Nowadays it seems like every other race of woman wants her bit of black, too. There was a time when white middle class women generally did not date black guys. Well, what would Mummy say? Now they can't wait to prove their right-on credentials.

Choices, choices, choices. So many choices. So many single women desperately seeking a partner. What is a guy to do? The answer is of course, 'his worst'.

The very reason why so many guys play the field is that the field is so *rahtid* wide and so accessible. Give a young boy the choice of any sweet in the candy store and the likelihood is he's gonna try and eat the whole lot! Unfortunately childhood tendencies are never that far away when it comes to the male mind. We tend to want to have our cake plus the whole bakery.

When inclination and opportunity meet, it often brings out the worst in anyone. This is the crux of the male dilemma in the new millennium. The desire to have it all and the opportunity to do just that. This abundance of choice has some bad implications for relationships. As a man it is too easy to treat relationships very casually. You don't need to commit yourself and put any great effort into it, because if you ain't happy, you can just chip and find the next woman who ain't gonna give you any grief.

In turn, women start to expect less from men and are more prepared to put up with nonsense. So many women I know are willing to allow their man to have a 't'ing on the side' because they see that as the norm.

Ultimately, having it all is never a good thing for a guy. You end up seeing women as disposable commodities and you never get a great deal out of relationships because you don't put that much into them in the first place. It really is like Burger King, we can have it our way.

"While it may be fun for a moment can you really play the same game for ever? Time to start answering that question, D. Seriously," Sweetie warned.

Yeah, yeah, yeah, but what about my balls?

WARNING:

THE NEXT CHAPTER IS STRICTLY FOR THE FELLAS.
LADIES, PLEASE MOVE ON TO THE CHAPTER AFTER
THE NEXT.

GAME, SET AND SNATCH YOUR BALLS BACK

RULES OF ENGAGEMENT
If you've recently lost your balls, please follow these simple rules and you won't go too far wrong.

RULE 1: Understand your 'prey'
When trying to get your balls back, study your prey, understand everything about her. Think of all the things a man is prepared to do to hang on to his balls, then remove logic, conscience and sense, and there you have a woman hanging on to your balls.

Women don't think like men, so don't expect them to. Women ain't simply men without willies, you know. There is a whole different set of values and thought processes going on there. You need to fully understand that before moving on.

Get a Saturday job in a women's hair salon to get a good insight into the ways of the woman's mind.

I suggest you invest in a good pair of binoculars,

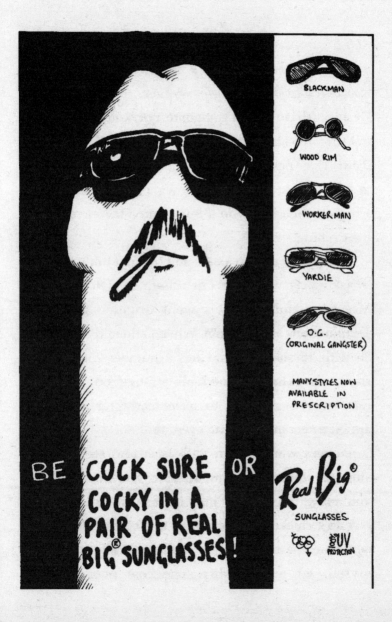

because your balls could be anywhere by now.

RULE 2: Get a nice car, job, and plenty of money/cash/dosh/wonga/spondoolies/benjies/ moolah/readies/digits/quids/pussytraps

Despite what women say about not being interested in the status and solvency of a man, we all know the truth. They never complain about being transported in a flash motor but just see how most will turn funny when you tell 'em, you'll buy them a travel card for the evening.

I once went out on a date and the first thing the gal is asking, is what car I'm rolling in. I told her a Mercedes and her eyes went brighter than the illuminations at Blackpool. When I added that it seats 36 with 16 standing and has a number 236 on the front, she kinda turned all strange on me and remembered she had to leave early for a dental appointment at ten in the evening.

Women want a man with cash and status. Full stop. Another important thing to remember before you blow the week's giro on a slap up meal at Nando's chicken emporium, is the 'cost over benefit equation'. To those not so mathematically adept as myself, let me simplify. The cost over benefit equation is simple: Will I get a good return for the money I'm investing in this project? Women will put out only after men have put out. You get me?

A word of warning. On no account overspend. It's the old, 'Well, I've already spent this much money' syndrome that catches so many guys out. The temptation is to keep spending money in some crazy attempt to hang on to your previous investment. I've seen too many guys sink more than the gross national product income of Bolivia into some foxy-looking babe because they are so determined to get their balls back they lose sight of reality. The wise guy knows when to cut his losses and leave the roulette table.

If you lack cash, status is a useful tool. Not everyone can be the managing director of a large multi-national but there is no reason why you can't up the status value of whatever job you do. A glass wall maintenance engineer sure as hell sounds more impressive than saying you're a window cleaner. Being vague is often a good idea.

My job? Oh I work in future risk analysis, behind the counter at a bookies.

A few quid spent at a printers getting some business cards made up with the title 'management consultant' will reap excellent returns.

RULE: 3 Be the loveable rogue

If there is one male personality type that is more or less guaranteed to have balls, it's the lovable bastard. Be too much Mister Nice Guy and babes will be totally disinterested. Come on too aggressive and they will chip just as quickly. The ideal is a combination of Mr Bad and Mr Good. 'Treat 'em mean to keep 'em keen' is an expression that is as old as Joan Collins, but there is a whole lot of truth in it.

And never appear too keen for sex. When you couldn't give a toss if you bed a woman or not, you're more or less guaranteed to get a result.

When it comes to getting laid, what works best for me is this letter that I've carried with me everywhere these past eight years:

Dear D, I still haven't fully recovered from last night. Even now my vagina is throbbing with ecstacy. You took me to places I have only fantasised about. I still can't believe how you rocked my world. Never before have I been made love to like you made love to me. I will never forget the way you touched my body and caressed me like a precious musical instrument, you took time to love me and discover all those secret places I had almost forgotten I possessed. Never in my wildest dreams did I imagine that my fantasies would ever be realised. You have fulfilled them all, and more. It's quite amazing. In your quest to satisfy me you took me, uninhibited, on a natural high. I never knew a woman could reach such heights. I have met men who have made me come, two, three or even four times, but to make me come every five minutes for hours... You worked your way inside me like an expert, and it seemed like every move you made was just right.

I don't know whether this is the beginning or the end (only time will tell what the future holds). If last night was only a moment that I am to share with you, then I am happy for that moment, because at last I have met a man whose sole intention is to please me, not just himself. Last night will remain a vivid memory.

It's going to be very hard to find someone to match up to you. I wish I could keep you, but I know that's not possible. I just had to let you know what you've done for me. And no matter what time of the day or night, you are welcome to rock my world and make me come EVERY and ANY time.　　　　　　　　　　*Yours M*

When I pull out that letter, women always say, "I wouldn't fall for that." Then they read it again, and again, and it stays on their mind until finally (it may take a week or two, a month at the most), when their curiosity is nearly killing them, they give in.

HARD AND STIFFIE

Dear Sweetie,

I regret to inform you that you have been eliminated from further contention to become the future Mrs. Adebayo. As you are probably aware, the competition was exceedingly tough this year and dozens of well-qualified candidates such as yourself also failed to make the final cut. I will, however, keep your name on file should an opening become available or I become extremely horny.

Sincerely,

D

Any sort of injury involving the testicles is not funny. Ladies have got to realise that a pain in the bollocks isn't going to make us laugh. My balls are very sacred to me. In fact my life depends on protecting them.

"So this is it?" Sweetie said.

It was nothing personal. Our relationship had passed its 'sell by' date. I wasn't about to shed any tears over it, but she was full of recrimination as she packed the few outfits and cosmetics she had stored at my place for those nights when she stayed over.

"You're sacking me to protect your balls?"

I simply nodded. Experience has taught me to get these things over and done with as quickly as possible and, for that, you need to avoid dialogue. And, besides, I knew what was coming next.

She said that one night of passion meant more to her than it does to me. I insisted that it meant less to me than it meant to me.

It used to be just the refrain of a pop song, but now guys everywhere are discovering that breaking up really is hard to do, especially when you're within the same time zone as the woman you're trying to dump. The closest most men come to telling a woman to her face that it's over, is to look her straight in the eye and say, "I'll call you next week."

Back in the day, men couldn't afford to leave their wives. Back then a man would pack his bags and announce, "I can't take no more, I'm leaving you," and his wife would say, "Okay, I'll see you later this evening when you get back."

In the eighties, women were positively insisting that their husbands should leave them. After all, she was leaving him behind socially, educationally, intellectually, economically and so on and so forth. She had a BSc and an MBA, and she was earning £50,000 a year more than him. Back then, guys would come home and find their bags packed and waiting for them, just because they didn't have a J-O-B not to talk of a degree. There are few things I find more distasteful than seeing a once dignified man reduced to a sobbing, blubbering heap, clinging onto the heels of his woman begging her: "Please, baby, PLEASE! Lawd, please don't throw me out. I'll cook for you, clean for you... I'll be your sex slave. Please, sweet jeeeeeezus, please, PLEEEZE!"

But a man who is prepared to settle down is so hard to find nowadays. Show me a woman today who encourages her man to leave let alone allows him to, and I'll show you a babe with a gigantic penis.

It ain't like the old days, y'know. Ask Lionel Richie, that light-skinned bruddah who used to sing, 'Hello, is it you I'm talking to...' When he tried to say 'good-bye' to his woman, he found that it wasn't so 'easy like Sunday morning'. No, sir, not at all. He ain't no light-skinned bruddah no more, neither. In fact, he's positively black and blue.

Guys, you can't be doing women like that any

Free at last! Free at last!! Free at last!!!

more and expect to walk away without a severe limp, a nose rammed deep in your cranium and several visits from the tooth fairy. This is the new millennium, you can't just walk out on a woman like you used to. At least wait until you can tell her over the phone, from the airport, as you're about to board that flight to an unknown destination, never to return until long after her death when you have finally overcome your inexplicable fear of duppies.

Woe betide the guy who chooses the checkout counter of some supermarket on a Saturday morning as the appropriate moment to tell his partner "A, B, see-yah!" But for some reason guys never listen to good advice. How often have we stood in line with our shopping, only to be held up by a woman losing her mind, determined by any means necessary to keep her man from walking out on her, knowing full well that if he does she may go to her grave single. How many times have we held our heads in shame as a woman loses her weave in a superstore and screams, "AAAAAGGHH, DON'T LEAVE, YOU DON'T KNOW ME, I'LL KILL YOU, I'LL KILL MYSELF, I'LL KILL EVERYBODY! NO, I WON'T KEEP MY VOICE DOWN, I DON'T CARE WHO HEARS. I DON'T WANNA BE LONELY!" As a volley of Heinz baked beans followed by cans of condensed milk rain down on the unsuspecting fellow.

It is a sad reflection on the state of love today that a woman has to resolve to actual and grievous bodily harm to keep her man. I would personally like to take this opportunity to apologize to the manager of Sainsbury's in Dalston, east London, for the 'circumstances beyond his control' that took place in the store last Saturday.

There was nothing I could do. Sweetie was hell-bent on a struggle/fight/mother of all battles/armageddon. She said I had used her and abused her until I used her up and that her 'bad karma' was going to get me.

That night I had a nightmare that she got busy with some garden shears while I was asleep. I have never had a dream so scary. For some unfortunate souls my worst nightmare becomes their reality.

For example, a bride in the town of Wuhu, eastern China, cut off her husband's penis while he slept. The woman, who obviously had limited experience of the male anatomy, told police that she believed it would grow back bigger than before. Makes you wonder what the hell they put in that special chop suey.

In 1995, a man of 67 who told New York police that

a vengeful hooker cut off his dick, eventually admitted he got careless with a carving knife. He made up the story because he was afraid that the truth would get him sent to the loony bin.

Another New Yorker, Earl Zea, aged 34, cut off his slong to discourage a male suitor, but told cops that an intruder had done it while he slept in his living room. The plod became suspicious after finding no blood stains. Zea was charged with falsely reporting an incident. "It's not against the law to remove your own penis," commented Fulton County District Attorney Polly Hoye.

Yanks must be seriously sick, because out in California this kind of shit is always happening. Alan Hall, 48, a pipe-fitter from Fairfield also told cops an elaborate story about how some angry woman had cut off his 't'ing'. After much wasting of police time, Hall admitted that he had mutilated himself with a hobby knife. He asked police not to disclose his motive.

Only in America..

NIGERIANS DO IT BETTER

Talking of America, Sweetie's Jamaican. Give her an inch and she'll want a Yardie, but she's now come to the conclusion that NIGERIANS DO IT BETTER.

For years it was Nigerians passing themselves off as yardies. Not just to avoid being branded a 'boo-boo' man but, most importantly, because the only way a Femi, Tunde or Dotun was going to stand a chance in chirpsing a fly-looking woman, was to walk like Shabba, talk like Shabba and to adopt the aka Leroy, Delroy, Glenroy or Trevva.

Back then, a guy didn't even have to look good. All he had to do was flash a gold tooth and promise to take her out to see a good "FLIM" and the woman would be like, "Ooh, you Jamaican guys are so sexy."

Guys didn't even need a modicum of intelligence. We didn't need to have two pennies to rub together. All we had to do was wear a Jamaican-flag string vest and say that we were from the 'land of wood...' and,

lo and behold, gals would rush us like water, little suspecting that we were from back-a-yard, Lagos.

On the streets of Peckham, they call us JAMAGERIANS.

Take my good friend Babatunde, aka Nigerian Dreddie, a true born Jamagerian. The best investment he ever made was in the 99 pence Jamaican-flag car sticker prominently displayed on his Datsun 'love machine' minicab. He claims that, since assuming Jamaican lineage, women have been going mad over his fresh 'Jamaican ketchup'.

Now, though, the 'original baby father-bandelero-gundelero-wicked-inna-bed-gal-'pon-consignment' tag has finally backfired on anybody of Jamaican descent with balls. After many frustrating years of waiting in vain for 'my Jamaican man' to commit in a one on one, rather than to a One2One, Jamaican women are turning their backs on yardies and flocking in droves to Nigerian men as their best chance of finding both a full-time father for their kids, and a husband to boot (though not literally).

It is now not uncommon at buppy parties to hear single women seeking a man, declaring: JAMAICANS NEED NOT APPLY.

Talk about Cool Britannia, Cool Nigerians more like!

You see, since discovering that Nigerian tradition

considers marriage to be 'non-negotiable' and children out of wedlock to be punishable by a severe flogging of their "irresponsible" father by his father / mother / grandfather / grandmother (whosoever wields the longest rod of correction), Sweetie realised that I was her best chance of finally standing in front of the pastor while I told the world how much I would love and cherish her.

For example, consider Ms T, a well-known television presenter who, unbeknown to her millions of admiring TV fans, has been miserable for the last few years since splitting up from her Jamaican partner and being left to bring up a child on her own. Looking more radiant than I had seen her in years, Ms T attended a champagne brunch I hosted recently, and quickly revealed that the cause of her sparkling demeanour was the new NIGERIAN man in her life. She said, the moment a genuine and bonafide no-kids-yet Nigerian with commitment came along, she jumped at a chance too good to miss. I expect to hear wedding bells shortly, but meanwhile she's determined to fulfil her TV commitments by being shot from the chest up, as she's already been blessed with a tiny little Nigerian in the oven.

Evelyn C is another example. A thirtysomething

single mother of three by three Jamaican men, she has turned her hand successfully to property speculation since her youngest daughter's father walked out the door and just kept on walking. She used to say she had given up completely on ever finding a "legitimate" man. However, she turned up at the brunch in triumphant mood, each hand clasping the bottom of one of a set of Nigerian twins (imaginatively christened Fola and Shola respectively).

Evelyn later confided in me that her orgasmic demeanour was due to having finally found a man who was prepared to "eat under a two foot table", and that she could now go to her grave happy.

As you can gather, things are looking pretty bad for the LATE GREAT JAMAICAN MALE. So bad, indeed, that Jamaican men are now passing themselves off as Nigerians, just to get a chance to chirps a quality woman. Even Nigerian Dreddie has swapped his car sticker for a Nigerian flag, and has reverted to calling himself Babatunde.

Me? Well, I've just come back from the dentist, where I joined a long line of JAMAGERIANS, all of us waiting to have our gold teeth pulled out.

NEVER MIND THE QUALITY

Does size matter? Apparently it didn't, until I gave
Sweetie her P45 and she felt it necessary to
shamelessly paste an unfavourably reduced
photocopy of my manhood on every lamp post in
Brixton.

Women can be so cruel. Blokes suffer from
manuncontrollabus sexulitis. But women suffer a
female equivalent of the ailment (*longdonkeydickis
irresistibillus*), and seem determined to make
sensitive guys like myself suffer for their malady.

I remember when most women were too coy about
admitting their darkest sexual fantasies to their
partners. Back then women would be like, "It's not
the size, it's what you do with it that counts." But
then along came Lunchbox Christie and, since then,
it's been "never mind the quality, feel the width, the
length, the circumference..."

Sweetie always maintained that she enjoyed my

company because of my charm and wit and 'other worldliness', which suited me down to the ground because I couldn't wait to sample her delights, either. When this woman talked dirty after dark, she was simply irresistible — the kind of woman that guys would cut their right arms off for. It wasn't just the horny words (for all I knew she was speaking Congolese), it was the way she moved her mouth when she said them. Even now my loins tremble when I think of what she could do for a man with a mouth like that.

But, hey, I'm just an average guy and, alas, Sweetie kept comparing me to her ex-boyfriend. Richard was a sagittarius and, by all accounts, half-man half-horse.

"I almost collapsed the first time he whipped it out," she commented casually on our first date. "It was the longest, thickest, meanest... the grandaddy of 'em all. All I could do was laugh and say, 'Where do you think you're going with that? No, not tonight sunshine...' "

How can women be so cold as to compare a guy to a horse? Don't you know that the size of a guy's cock is a symbol of his male virility, part and parcel of his erotic mythology, proof of his very existence? That's why we keep grabbing our crotches, because women have taken nearly everything else from us, it seems like that's one of the few things we've got left!

Moreover, Richard was a yank!

I told Sweetie in no uncertain terms what I thought of her ex. "Oh sure, on the surface those Yank guys look all groomed and sophisticated, but when yah dig a little deeper you soon find that:

1. They are more likely to detect prostrate cancer than us. So many of them have their heads up the appropriate place, that they know their bottoms like we know the back of our hands.

2. Everything is bigger in America. That includes bellies. The average American man consumes as many calories in a day as the entire population of Addis Ababa. Yanks eat food like it was going to be banned tomorrow. The average British guy thinks about sex every eight minutes. American men just eat every minute.

3. They talk a good talk. Sure do. Americans certainly have the gift of the gab. Only a Yank could say 'I love history, it's just so old' or 'I wanna visit Britain

because everyone speaks American' and not realise what a complete prat he is.

4. Yanks know how to treat a woman like a lady. The men are as tough as a big girl's blouse. They lost their balls ages ago, and are so close to being women themselves that they can better relate to being one. Behind all the front, the average Yank geezer has as much backbone as a jellyfish. One bomb going off in Europe has them running to hide under the bed in Atlanta."

Despite insisting that she wanted to forget all about Richard and his gigantic phallus, Sweetie's world seemed to be littered with reminders. If I fancied munching on a banana sundae, she would comment that Richard's motto was: 'Think big, think plantain'. When we saw an advertising billboard with a witch on a broomstick, she remembered how Richard was so long and strong that she could 'ride' him with no visible means of support. Nelson's column brought back fond memories, as did the time we happened to be picnicking on a conspicuous hillside at Cerne Abbas in Dorset, where a colossal chalk-cut figure of a giant was made 2000 years ago by early anglo-

It's a fact. Men love dicks.

saxons, with a spectacularly erect 30 foot penis rising up in the centre of its body!

It's not the kind of thing a man wants to discuss with his close male friends, yet what was I to do? Women don't mind going to the doctor for every little embarrassing problem, but guys would sooner die of ignorance. Fortunately, my good friend Lenny is a man's man, a spar's spar. The kind of guy you can do your male bonding with without feeling awkward. A knowledgeable man with good advice to impart to his brotherman.

"Oh, you're simply suffering from an acute dose of *cockshrivelupagus* to give it its correct latin name," Lenny informed me. "Loosely translated, it's a burning desire to possess an extremely large phallus. Until you develop a bedroom bully to match Richard's, you will always feel like a little pussy..."

Lenny advised me to take out an immediate subscription to *Penis Power Monthly*, an absorbing American publication. "However, if you want immediate results," he continued, "you have basically two options: There is a popular form of erotic surgery in the Philippines, where small plastic balls called *bulitas* are inserted beneath the skin to enlarge the penis for added sexual pleasure for the ladies and sheer PAIN for the men..."

Needless to say, that option received little consideration. Lenny agreed that a guy shouldn't have to go *that* far to satisfy his woman. So, Option 2:

"There's this doctor who has made a fortune with his penis enlargement operation. It's like liposuction in reverse. He takes fatty tissue from elsewhere on the body and injects it into the penis to increase its girth, while the length is increased by releasing two inches of manhood normally held inside the body. The operation takes about 40 minutes under general anaesthetic and costs five grand and (surprise, surprise), the good doctor has no shortage of patients — he gets 2,000 enquiries a day and the waiting list is six months. I can personally vouch for the operation, because I used to be average, around 6 inches... Now I've got 9 inches, and that's a power buzz — no need for a flash car."

I have to admit that I did go to the surgeon and tell him to double the size of my dick. He looked at me with a shocked expression and said. "What the hell are you going to do with a 24 inch penis?" I'm telling you, that's the way it happened!

Which is just as well, as Lenny admitted that there were horror stories to consider:

"I never go overseas on holiday, because the operation increases the likelihood of a penis explosion — particularly during a trans-Atlantic flight, due to cabin pressure..."

Such option put the whole thing in perspective.

Anyway, it's not the male size that matters. If a woman is 'the right size', even a miniscule penis can feel huge.

SADDEST BASTARD OF THE 20th CENTURY

When poor Gerhard van der Merwe fell out of the big dick tree he missed every branch. You see Gerhard who is aged 22 was, until very recently, sporting a wood all of two and a half inches long. I say 'recently' because thanks to the miracles of modern surgery, he's just had an operation to double the size of his plonker.

South African Gerhard, has been badly under-endowed since birth. Explains mum Gloria, "When the midwife brought him to me for the first time, I saw straight away that my little boy wasn't quite right." (Nor quite left).

Gerhard says he was five or six, (years not inches), when he realised he didn't quite look like the other chaps. "I saw they had something I didn't. I've been

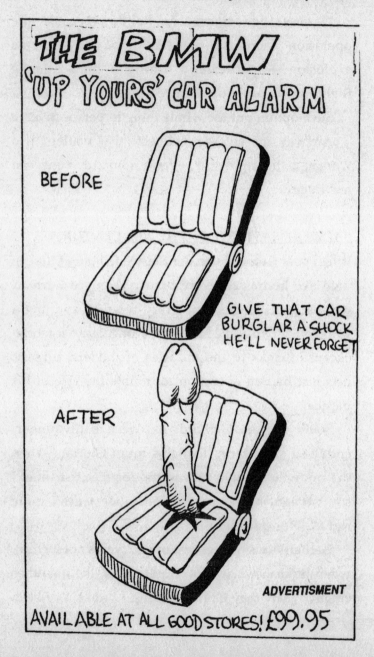

ashamed all my life. At school when other boys came into the urinal, I would turn away so that they couldn't see."

Gerhard's pathetic story was featured in the black South African magazine *Drum*, and it must have provided much mirth for the readership. I can imagine there were a few brothas who went to work with a bit more of a swagger in their walk and a grin on their faces, after reading that article.

What I can't imagine is what would possess a man to go and tell the world that his dick is so tiny he had to have an operation to bring it up to 'small'. This guy is endowed all right, he must be one of the world's biggest dickheads going.

While on this subject, yes, I really do have a twelve inch willy, but I don't use it as a rule. Now don't misunderstand, or as they say in China "don't get me Wong," there is everything right with realising there is more to life than the size of your dick. A huge dong doesn't make you a better person, I should know.

It's like those guys who seem to think that gold plating their dong will enhance it's attractiveness. Even when women smirk and laugh under their breath these sad guys just don't seem to see that they might, just perhaps, look like a complete prat.

NEW MILLENNIUM WOMAN

Dear D,
Men like you are: out of date, out of time, out of step, out
of your minds and out of a job. Or haven't you heard, the
women are doing it for themselves...
*   S.O.S. (Swing Out Sistas), Tottenham.*

Women have been telling us for years that, in the new
millennium, men will no longer be so damn relevant,
that our services will not be required and that our
functions will be redundant, unless we shape up and
make up for a thousand years of disrespect. Like any
man about to get sacked, you can't blame me and the
fellas for losing our heads trying to get as much out
of the job as possible, even if it means shafting the
boss, and her mates, too.

I mean, up until now gender roles have been
clearly defined — women do all the hard work and
suffer all the heartaches, while men provide (most of)

the sweetness, and in times of war sacrifice their lives (or in disasters such as the sinking of the *Titanic*, allow women and children off the ship first). Yet, a guy can't go anywhere nowadays without some woman reminding you that 'time's up' and that, thanks to the appliance of science, women will no longer be slaves to the male phallus and will, henceforth, not be spending the rest of their lives in usage, bondage and abusage.

"We won't be the same fools in the new millennium as we've been in the last one," Sweetie assured me. "Women are through with the twentieth century man — the jerk, the con man, the sleazy lover, the skeezer, the geezer, the charming scoundrel, married seducer, mama's boy, batterer, critic, addict and serial baby father."

(I guess that rules us all out, fellas.)

The new millennium woman will be able to do it all by herself, Sweetie claims. She'll be able to conceive by simply clicking her fingers. She'll be father, mother, sister, brother, uncle, aunt, grandmother and grandfather to her child, and to herself she can be a lover, too.

Thanks to science, the D.I.Y. woman of the future will not have to turn on her charm every time she needs a little soldering. She won't need a man to teach her how to drive (properly), and when it comes to those lonely nights when she's in a cold sweat dreaming about having a man right there beside her to hold and caress, to sip a glass of chilled champagne with, and to whisper sweet-nothings in her ear, the new millennium woman will be able to reach for her automatic, push-button, remote controlled, all-action throbbing, knobbing computer chip with a massive wood. Apparently, this new twelve-inch variable speed, latex product is able to keep going for many more hours than any man.

While I have no doubt that science can create a substitute caucasian male, I think you'll find that the negro male is an entirely different species — we just can't be packaged and sold willy nilly (oops).

Despite new millennium science and technology, some things will remain the same: though men will have more hair than women, on the hole women will have more than men.

WHAT DO WOMEN WANT?

a faithful boyfriend.

a great body.

eating without gaining weight.

unlimited credit cards.

commitment.

looking great in a bikini.

diamonds.

more diamonds.

gossip

more gossip

romantic movies with sad endings.

guys who dance well.

no-calorie pizza.

revenge.

men to have a period — just ONCE.

not having to shave.

guys that smell good.

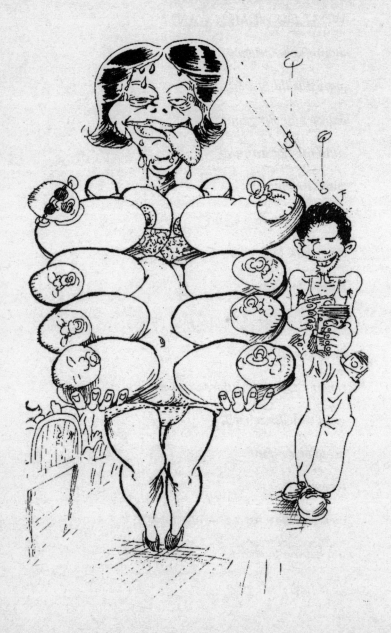

reading guys' minds.

reading other women's minds.

expensive things.

love at first sight.

L-O-N-G hot baths.

countless pairs of shoes.

flattery.

going up a bra size.

flowers.

honest guys who know when to lie.

men with good, strong, hands.

a good horoscope.

sentimental moments.

memorable kisses.

inspiring jealousy.

a secret admirer.
great back massages.

DON'T BELIEVE THE HYPE

With every other newspaper article about Viagra these days, you could be forgiven for assuming that all men suffer from impotency. Don't you believe it. According to a recent medical report a large number of geezers don't have a problem loading their rifles they have trouble stopping the gun going off too quickly.

Yes, premature ejaculation is apparently a big problem for many men. How it's a problem I don't know. I mean, if you come in thirty secs or twenty minutes, what's the difference? Either way you've had a good time, right? As far as I can see, premature ejaculation can never be a problem for a man, although his women may see things differently.

Spring time again and love is in the air. Single women are once again resorting to any means necessary to find a man and drag him to the church on time. I recently heard of one thirtysomething female

JUST FOR THE
TASTE OF IT.

architect who raised her own dowry of some £30,000. Needless to say, she's now happily married to the man of her choice. If there's one thing that never fails to prompt a man to say 'I do', it's a cash incentive.

Marriage is good, but it's not that good, I hear you say. Because most women with thirty grand at their disposal would rather spend it on hair products. Women nowadays tend to favour a 'no fee' wedding arrangement. For instance, I know guys who claim they didn't know what they were doing when they walked down that aisle, that they were not fully *cockus mensus*. I personally am not suggesting they were drugged, but they are...

Some women won't even business with slipping some 'love potion No.9' into a guy's Dragon Stout and pussywhipping their way up to the altar. Frankly, there is nothing I find more distasteful than to see a guy led to his wedding on a leash, with his tongue hanging to the ground and panting heavily all because of he's lost his balls. What was it that Beenie Man was saying about "old dogs like we"? It's true, all men are dogs. It's just that some are rottweilers like me, and some are chihuahuas. And it takes more than whip appeal to get a rottweiler to utter those marriage vows.

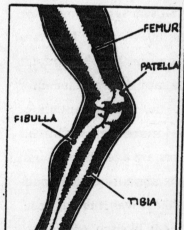

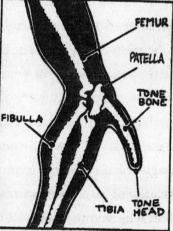

Men are dogs, women are spiders. And not just any old spider, but that classic trickster Anansi who never gives up. Once she's got her eye on a certain guy, it's all over. Signed, sealed, delivered — rings on her fingers, bells on her toes and a marriage certificate safely tucked into her spider's web. Sista Anansi don't ramp.

Sista Anansi is prepared to lie her way to a white wedding. And, let's face it, when it comes to telling whoppers the women have had a lot of practice. From back in the raving days when, instead of giving you their home number, they would write down the number of the local Chinese takeaway or Battersea Dog's Home on the back of a sincere guy's hand. Or leave you standing in the rain at Leicester Square for a date at eight which they had no intention of making. And when guys are fortunate enough to get a date with a 'stush' woman and we tell 'em straight from the beginning that we don't want a serious relationship, women will be like, "Yeah, neither do I," when they know full well that they are lying.

Amongst the most memorable lies that women come up with are the Wonderbra (for guys to wonder where it's all gone when they see you naked the next morning), and the Miracle Boost Denims aka the

Bottom bra aka the Bum bra.

Then there's that BIG lie women seem to enjoy so much. You know, the one that keeps the neighbours up half the night: 'Yessss....ooooohhh YESSSSSSSS...OOOHHHH YES! YES!! YEEEEEESSSS...!!!' And it's always the same punchline: "You're such a brilliant lover, you make me come every time."

Ladies, if you want a satisfying sex life, you will NEVER fake an orgasm. How d'you expect guys to believe a single word you say when you'll make up any old story just to be 'legit'?

Now Sweetie expects me to believe that she's pregnant! Yeah, *right!* Ladies, you think that guys still fall for that old chestnut? This is the new millennium, baby. Pregnant *indeed!* Is nothing sacred anymore?

She reckons she's going to have a pregnancy test. Yeah, *right!* I might even play along with her for a bit, just to humour her. What the hell, I might even throw in a couple of quid towards the Predictor...

FAKING IT

Womanspeak: We need.

Translation: I want.

Womanspeak: Do what you want.

Translation: You'll pay for this later.

Womanspeak: We need to talk.

Translation: I need to complain.

Womanspeak: I'm hungry.

Translation: Stop whatever you are doing, scrape together your last fiver, and drive across town and get me something to eat.

Womanspeak: I'm not upset.

Translation: Of course I'm upset, you idiot.

Womanspeak: You're so manly.

Translation: You need a shave and you sweat a lot.

Womanspeak: You're certainly attentive tonight.

Translation: Is sex all you ever think about?

Womanspeak: I'm not emotional! And I'm not overreacting!

Translation: I've got my period.

Womanspeak: The bin is full.

Translation: Take it out.

Womanspeak: The dog is barking.

Translation: Go outside in your underwear and see if a burglar is trying to break in.

Womanspeak: Hang the picture there.

Translation: NO, I mean hang it there!

Womanspeak: Do you love me?

Translation: I'm going to ask for something expensive.

Womanspeak: How much do you love me?

Translation: I've done something you're not going to like.

Womanspeak: I'll be ready in a minute.

Translation: Kick off your shoes and find a good game on TV.

Womanspeak: Is my bottom fat?

Translation: Tell me I'm beautiful.

Womanspeak: You have to learn to communicate.

Translation: Just agree with me.

Womanspeak: Are you listening to me?!

Translation: Too late, you're dead.

Womanspeak: It's all right, dear.

Translation: You'll pay for this.

Womanspeak: Yes.

Translation: No.

Womanspeak: No.

Translation: No.

Womanspeak: Maybe.

Translation: No.

Womanspeak: Was that the baby?

Translation: Why don't you get out of bed and walk him until he goes to sleep?

Womanspeak: Do you like this dish?

Translation: It's an easy to fix recipe so you'd better get used to it.

Womanspeak: I'm sorry.

Translation: You'll be sorry.

Womanspeak: Who's driving?

Translation: You're driving.

Womanspeak: So is she pretty?

Translation: The correct answer is NO.

Womanspeak: I don't want to talk about it.

Translation: Go away, I'm still building up steam.

Womanspeak: Nothing.

Translation: Everything.

Womanspeak: All we're going to do is stop to pick up some milk.

Translation: It goes without saying that we're stopping at the cosmetics department, the shoe

department, I need to look at a few new pocket books, and 'OMIGOD' there's a sale in lingerie, and wouldn't these pink sheets look great in the bedroom and did you bring your checkbook?

Womanspeak: What's wrong? Nothing, really.

Translation: It's just that you're such an arsehole.

Womanspeak: I'm not yelling!

Translation: Yes I am yelling!

Womanspeak: What makes you think there is something wrong?

Translation: I'm going to cut off your balls, tonight. Don't spend lots of money on me.

Translation: I want the big, expensive one on the right.

Womanspeak: Don't you remember?

Translation: It was four years ago, and I've never forgiven you.

Womanspeak: Her smile is wonky.

Translation: Men think she's a sex goddess.

"Honey," said Sweetie, "what would you do if I died?"

"I would be extremely upset," I replied. "Why do you ask?"

"Would you have children with another woman?" she persevered.

H.M. GOVERNMENT WARNING: Womanspeak can seriously fuck you up.

"No, of course not," I said.

"Why not?"

"All right, then," I said, "I'll have more children with another woman."

"You would?" she said, looking hurt.

"Yes."

"Would you sleep with her in our bed?" Sweetie said, after a long pause.

"Well yes, I suppose I would."

"I see," she snapped. "And would you let her wear my clothes?"

"I suppose, if she wanted."

"Really," she said icily. "And would you take down the photos of me and replace them with pictures of her?"

"Yes. I think that would be the right thing to do."

"Is that so? And I suppose you'd let her play my guitar, too."

"Of course not, Sweetie," "she's left handed... Aaaaaaaaaaaagh, my baaaaaaaaaaaaaaalls!!!!!!!!!"

Nothing Sweetie says or does surprises me any more. If any university out there is planning research into the mating rituals of the female and needs a learned authority to head up the project, I'm your man. Gizza job, I could do that.

It's been my life's work to observe and record the strange habits of this perplexing species. The following are, in no particular order, three random recurring scenes in that long, wide screen movie called 'The Mating Game'.

SCENE 1:

You're single again. You've met a woman a fortnight ago and you're out on your second date. Three hours later the two of you are back at your yard banging harder that a blacksmith at his anvil. What I always find strange about this scene is that during dinner, when you were wondering if she was gonna be worth the £30 food investment, she tells you that the last time she had sex was eighteen months ago.

What's strange is that every woman I've met 'last had sex' eighteen months previously. Now I don't wanna be calling you no liar, girlfriend, but it does kinda seem odd how every gal has the same time span. So how does that work then? I mean, as a woman do you suddenly start to feel horny exactly eighteen months after you last had it? Do you suddenly feel the urge so bad that you just gotta have? What I always think is such an amazing coincidence is that I constantly meet women at the end of their long bout of enforced celibacy. Isn't that incredible?

If for one moment, one entertained the idea that perhaps some of these women were being economical with the truth, what reason could there be for such falsehoods? Does it appear immoral to men to say that you last had a good service a week ago, or even three days prior? Is this the reasoning? Does a year seem too short, and two years too round a number? Is that where the eighteen month term comes in? Please, ladies, share your secrets and let us know.

All I can say is that, it does stretch most guys gullibility just a bit too much. I mean, here you are spanking the booty on only your second date, yet you have been saving it all for me, Mr Loverman.

Hell, I might have an ego but it ain't the size of Alaska, baby!

SCENE 2:
You're staring open-mouthed at the bill in front of you. The waiter's smirking. This honey that you've just met is used to doing everything in style. She has to eat at the best restaurants and she hangs at the best clubs. She doesn't drink anything but the best

champagne. Guess who is going to end up funding her lavish ways? How come, when you eventually end up at her shabby council high-rise, you see no evidence of this jetset lifestyle she tells you she lives? The LEB power key on the table makes you wonder how she can afford to travel to New York on Concorde just to go shopping.

SCENE 3:

Guys, is the woman you're seeing hot in bed? Ever wondered how she got that way? Me too. 'Cause all the women I've ever dated have told me they ain't had more than five sexual partners in their life and they are fairly inexperienced. But come the time you whip out the handcuffs and start to read the locking instructions on the box, she's clicking them around your wrists at a speed that would put an arresting police officer to shame. How do you ladies adapt so quickly to things you've never done before? How do you do that?

According to a recent women's magazine survey, 75% of female respondents admitted that they had faked orgasms. Sweetie claims she was one of them.

I'm under no illusions about the acting abilities of

some women out there. Believe. From my own limited experiences of such matters, I've been with women that, in a fair world, should have been rushing up those steps on Oscar night to pick up their award for best supporting actress. And Sweetie's one of them.

I would never in my wildest ego trips assume that I was able to get my woman to the moon every time. So long as she is happy, I don't hurt my ego to know that she ain't having an orgasm every time.

But why do women feel the need to fake it? According to Michael Castleman, author of the book, *Sexual Solutions: A Guide For Men And The Women Who Love Them*, the most cited reasons by women are 'to avoid accusations of unresponsiveness, to bolster the man's ego, or to end a sexual experience they would like to conclude'.

I've heard 'nuff guys bragging about the size of their wood and how they can stay on the job all night long. Well, if you're a man who falls into that camp, Castleman's words ain't gonna go down too tough. He says that many geezers think that all that is needed for a woman to reach orgasm is vaginal intercourse. And, of course, the more you do it and the harder you do, the quicker she'll get there.

If you don't satisfy her...some other guy will!

WHAT GUYS SAY, AND WHAT THEY REALLY MEAN

Manspeak: I don't know if I like her.

Translation: She won't blow me.

Manspeak: I really want to get to know you better.

Translation: So I can tell my friends about it.

Manspeak: How do I compare with all you other boyfriends?

Translation: Is my penis really that small?

Manspeak: I want you back.

Translation: For tonight anyway.

Manspeak: I miss you so much.

Translation: I am so horny that my flatmate is starting to look good.

Manspeak: No, I do not want to dance right now.

Translation: Because I have a hard-on.

Manspeak: The break-up should start in 24 hours.

Translation: I want sex with you a few more times.

Manspeak: I am different from all the other guys.

Translation: I am not circumcised.

FREAKY

The first Jamaican vibrator? I can just see the advert:

The Supa Yardie comes complete with mains adaptor and 18" extension. Soon come? She will with a Ronco Supa Yardie.'

But why is it that satisfying a woman's sexual fantasies has got to be so hard on my throat, not to mention the knees? To women it might be kinky, but ask any guy who's tried to perform oral sex while hanging upside down from the chandeliers, hardcore porn is better.

You give a bunch of guys a handful of dirty magazines and a video and they can entertain themselves all weekend. Yet men are made to feel like perverts for reading girlie magazines. Reach for the top shelf and the Asian newsagent tries to match your profile with the mug shots in the latest sex offender list.

But, hey, I'm not the only guy who finds girlie

THE OFFICIAL BED-ROOM BULLY HANDSHAKE

magazines erotic. I don't know a single man out there who hasn't got a secret stash of 'em hidden behind the immersion heater or up in the loft. Especially the 'lifers' (husbands in marriages from which there is no escape).

Don't get me wrong, I've got nothing against kinky underwear. I've got some on right now as a matter of fact... Besides, the g-string, the batty rider and the punny printer are better than those high-waisted granny panties women used to wear with bras you could measure the length of your garden with.

What attracted me to Mrs XXX when she moved in next door and popped round to borrow some coffee, was that she claimed that her husband left her because she was too kinky and that in the fifteen years she had been married to Mr XXXX, there was still only one kinky thing he wouldn't perform on her — being Jamaican and all.

It seemed only natural that we should retire to my bedroom. I went to change into something a little more comfortable — black leather boots with eight-inch heels, a leather miniskirt, a rubber bra with the nipples cut out, a dog collar and a leather hood. I grabbed a riding crop and some handcuffs and sauntered out seductively, only to catch Mrs XXX as she was about to leave.

"Where are you going," I asked, "I thought we were about to get kinky?"

"Hey," she said, "I've pissed in your sink and I've given your dog a blow job... What more do you want?"

Two words, ladies: blow job. Learn it. Live it. LOVE IT.

Picture the scene: Your man is sitting in the armchair daydreaming with a sly grin around his chops. You ask him what he's thinking about and he says "Oh, nothing" and then focuses his attention on the telly. Sounds familiar? Ever wondered what he was really thinking about?

Well, allow me to enlighten you about the workings of the male mind. If a man ain't thinking about food (he would definitely tell you if he was), then he's thinking about sex. Now if you want to know specifically what aspect of puntang his mind is focused on then check this out:

THE TEN MOST POPULAR MALE FANTASIES

1. The Threesome

You could be forgiven for thinking that ménage à trois was a kind of vegetable but no, this is a whole lot more enjoyable than a plate of greens. The idea of sex with two women is quite frankly most guys' top fantasy. Apparently the ultimate threesome fantasy for the blokes interviewed is for a guy to have sex doggy style while the women perform oral sex on each other. Oh yeah? And I'd like a Ferrari for Christmas too! Sounds like these blokes have been watching too many porno movies.

2. The Oral Sex Thang

To quote *Today's Black Woman* magazine, 'many brothers said they fantasise about having oral sex with their wives and girlfriends and having them reciprocate'. Rhatid! Black American men must be as straight in bed as Jamaicans. Oral sex a fantasy? I always thought it was a regular part of the show myself. Apparently the brothas interviewed claimed that the reason they sometimes dated white women was because black women were 'old fashioned' in this regard. I've heard some excuses in my time, but this one... I can't think who these 'old fashioned' black women are. From my experience, if you ain't 'going there' you ain't gonna get any where.

3. The 'Mile High Club'

Many brothas fantasise about having sex on an aeroplane says the survey. Load of bollocks. Most men I know fantasise about a woman buying them an airline ticket!

4. The 'Pretzel' Fantasy

When I saw the title of this fantasy I thought it was about putting snacks in places other than the kitchen cupboard. But apparently it means the fantasy about having sex in a multitude of positions. Men complained that the missionary position is "tired and has played out." Once again if this is defined as a fantasy then all I can say is Yanks must be as adventurous in their sexual technique as Marks & Spencer are in their knitwear design.

5. Spontaneous Sex

Like Martini, any time any place, is what men want. In the kitchen, on the floor, in the hall, in your best friend's bedroom (with preferably your best friend).

6. Sex In the Shower

A good clean fun fantasy this one. Could be a little difficult to act out if you only have a bath in your house. But with a bit of string and a watering can, anything is possible.

7. The Character Fantasy

Always a popular one, be it pretend policewomen, nurses of domestic workers. You know the one. The missus gets dressed up in a Victorian maid's outfit and comes into 'Sir's' room to dust. The cheeky wench is then bent over Sir's antique MFI melamine card table and giving a damn good...

8. The Slut/Bad Girl

Another favourite sexual fantasy that men want to experience is having wild, nasty sex with the bad girl — the one they would never dream of bringing home to meet mum. She is the epitome of the slut: she will do anything and do it well. Some guys are seriously into this one. Rather like my mate Keith who went and married his. Keith, I'm only joking son, I really don't think your woman's that much of a slag.

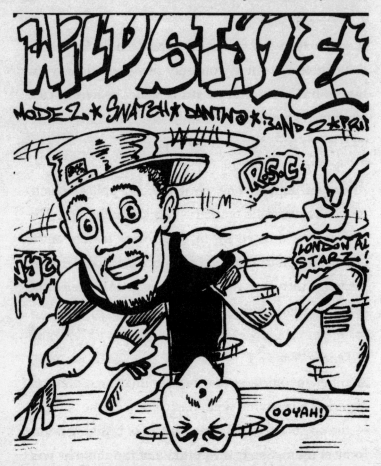

SEX ON THE DANCEFLOOR

9. Forbidden Fruit

Men always want what they can't/shouldn't have. The forbidden fruit is often the one that tastes sweetest. The forbidden fruit could be women of other races, married women — especially those married to friends and relatives.

10. Sex In Public

Many men fantasise about having sex in a park, in a lift, telephone box etc. This is an easy one for most Londoners to fulfill. It gets so crowed on the Underground these days that you're practically having sex with the person next to you anyway. The other morning I was pushed up against some secretaries from Liverpool Street all the way to Notting Hill. The fact I only needed to travel one stop is neither here nor there.

Some of these so-called fantasies are so limp that you really must question the imagination and sexually repressed nature of our Yank brothas. For guys who like to think of themselves as hot Denzil Washington studs, these yanks seem to be about as wild as a day trip to Hastings. Come on guys where are the frogman suits, the jar of honey, surgical gloves, dead chicken, fireman's boots, sailor's rope and large cucumber?

But who am I to diss our transatlantic cousins? The fact of the matter is that men over here are probably just as reserved as most seats on an inter city to Birmingham. I do hear a number of black women saying that white guys can hump and are a whole lot more freaky with it. At the same time they say that black guys are not as imaginative as they could be.

ANOTHER MALE FANTASY: BODY BEAUTIFUL

Ladies, it has recently come to my attention that an increasing number of you have been spending too much time on your brains while neglecting your bodies.

Like guys really care if you're a chess grandmaster with a PhD from Oxford.

For hundreds of years, men have been consumed by the quest for the perfect female body, that elusive '10'. Like so many other of my male counterparts, I am always being unfairly accused of sleeping around when all I'm doing is continuing the search so that mankind may someday find that jackpot. So far I've only managed to find a 9, so, alas, altruistic guys like myself have to continue going out of our way from bed to bed and from butt-naked woman to butt-naked woman all in the name of this small quest for man, this giant-like hunt for mankind.

In a recent survey, a handful of my bonafide breddahs voted black MP Oona King 'the thinking man's crumpet'. The problem is, there ain't a whole lot of thinking guys out there, apart from those of us who are thinking 'Where the booty at?' or 'Where the loot at?'

In my experience, when it comes to women's bodies, there's always room for improvement. Trust me, I'm something of an expert on the matter. Ladies, allow me to give you a second opinion, please. I'll even throw in the number of a good Harley Street consultant. If he can turn Michael Jackson into a white man, he'll have no trouble transforming your jelly roll into the perfect body.

Because thanks to the advancements in modern cosmetic surgery, women can order a new body just as easily as a pizza/having her hair done/her nails manicured. All you've got to do is click your fingers and you, too, can cause a major traffic pile-up (at least you won't be in it, now that you've traded your cabriolet for your body beautiful).

You don't even have to be pretty. You can be ugly as hell. Guys will simply shrug their shoulders and say, "Shame about the face, but GREAT body! I wonder if she'll hold it against me..."

Ladies, no offence, but when a man puts a woman on a pedestal he expects her to go down on it.

When I say "GREAT body," I'm willing to accommodate all shapes and sizes, as long as they're built for comfort and not built for speed, in fact a little extra weight looks good.

Women keep their bodies looking good while they're trying to catch a man. But as soon as he's hooked line and sinkered, many women stop going to the gym. Then they've got the cheek to turn around and ask, "Honey, does my batty look big in this?"

"Compared to what? I've seen bigger and I've seen smaller," is my reply.

When it comes to sex, nothing makes a man want to hurry up and get it over with quicker than a lazy body just lying there studying a crack in the ceiling. A body so tired that you have to wake it up and inform it that you've finished. The kind of body that's always too hot, too sore, not in the mood, wrong time of the month and even pretends to be asleep. The kind of body that's always praying that all other women's bodies are heavier than it is....

Women are also looking for a man with a great

body. That's why they don't go for that big fat guy in the Fresh Prince of Bel Air. Unfortunately for the ladies, though, those male models with perfect bodies are all gay. And whereas guys are honest enough to say that we're on a mission to find that elusive '10', women act like they prefer Wesley for aesthetic reasons, that they are conducting research for their degree and that brains come before beauty in the black women's world.

Purleeeeeaaaze!

A beautiful body is a fine work of art, but if you're looking for a '10', you'll forget the Tate and the National galleries and your Monets and your Picassos, if you want me to talk about really fine, priceless art, ladies, you're going to have to lift up your blouses, because I can't see.

Forget the sex toys and the kinky lingerie, there's nothing that will turn your man on more than a 'No Entry' sign subtly tattooed across your buttocks. Ladies, why bother to go and get your hair done and your nails done, when all you've got to do to drive your man wild and wicked inna bed is simply go and get your neck done, or your thigh done, or a nose-ring, tongue stud, nipple ring or other ornament pierced through the most intimate of places. Why, I know one Caribbean queen with her last will and testament tattooed on her back, who makes a good living showing her impressionist body art off to truckloads of orgasmic men, and I'm not talking about the rings on her eyelids, either.

You see, body art is the 'in thing'. So, forget your smooth and unblemished skin, and dash 'way your gold tooth and your pretty face (what sexual satisfaction can guys get from that?) A strategically well-placed tattoo, on the other hand, increases sexual attractiveness so much so, that whenever I see a female tattoo, I always feel like accidently grabbing some woman's backside — any woman's.

Tattooing is as old as time and was certainly turning men on as far back as the Stone Age, when they were thought to protect the bearer from evil spirits. Still today, in the islands of the South Pacific, a tattoo on a woman is considered very desirable, especially attractive and a sign that the bearer will be better able to cope with the pain of childbirth. Over here though, it's a promise of raw, unadulterated, hot and kinky sex.

Only a few years ago, no self-respecting woman would even consider subjecting herself to the excruciating pain of body decoration/mutilation.

Can I have my balls back please?

"No man, the one on the right is yours!"

Nowadays, however, women with cash have been avail themselves regularly of the services of the local 'body artist'. Yeah, if you've got the cash, then go and see the plastic surgeon to re-design your tits, but I wouldn't risk going on a charter flight afterwards as silicone has a habit of exploding under cabin pressure. Whereas body piercing and tattooing are safe, reliable and (so far) require only a minimum of genetic modification.

You see, a strategically placed tattoo is another way of saying "I will make a good sexual partner". 'Cause at the end of the day, that's all a guy is interested in. Meeting eager-to-please, open-minded sex partners is our main hobby in life. As I've always maintained, if there was a way of telling the good sexual partners apart from the others, men wouldn't have to waste so many years of our lives reluctantly enduring one night stands as we search in vain for that perfect partner. You get me?

This fact has not been lost on those ugly women who, back in the day, always went everywhere with a woman who was even uglier, to make them look better and draw the negative attention away from their flaws and onto someone else's (Men sometimes use this trick as well. I know, because I used to spar with the model Elo). These same ugly women now have tattoos screaming atcha from the top of their breasts in low-cut blouses and, nowadays, go raving and love to be seen with women who would never in a million years contemplate getting their noses pierced, let alone a tattoo. Us guys ain't stupid, trust me. We know which one is going to give it up good, and we don't care how ugly she is. It's called blind curiosity and all guys can think about is, "If she's got the bottle to get that tattoo done, imagine what she's going to be like in bed! Yeeeeeaaagghhh!!!"

However much you think you're having a satisfactory sex life, ladies, check your friends with the body art and you might discover that they're having an even more satisfactory (longer, leaner, meaner and more regular) sex life.

Not having a tattoo on display nowadays is almost like saying, 'I am frigid'. I mean, just about the only woman who hasn't got a tattoo is YOU and one or two confirmed spinsters of the church who believe that all forms of body decorations are insults to God, who has designed mankind the way he wanted them.

IN SEARCH OF GOODPUSSY

Like someone once said, "All is fair in love and war." I use every trick in the book to get laid. In search of sexual gratification, even men with the highest morals and most esteemed social status are prepared to see how low they can go. But wait, there are certain tricks that I am not particularly proud of.

Lack of libido control is one of them. A problem that most men are inflicted with. I learned it as a teenager, in those nine month gaps when you begin to seriously doubt whether you'll ever get laid again (ever), and now I've got it down to a fine art. It's not as simple as saying that my brain resides in my Calvin Kleins. Nor is it just a case of my penis being a Ferrari substitute. It's more complicated than that. Think of the Pied Piper and all those kids following him to their doom and you'll be closer to the truth. Because once that old refrain starts playing, there are very few things that men will not do in the eternal quest for goodpussy.

The first time I risked life and limbs in my search for sexual satisfaction, I was still a choirboy. Only sixteen years old, I couldn't believe my luck when I lost my virginity to seventeen year old Jackie P, who later revealed that her ex-boyfriend was the insanely jealous Ricky H, the school's best fighter and a certified psychopath. It was common knowledge that Ricky would personally crucify anybody who dared to check for Jackie. He spent his woodwork classes building a life-size replica of the cross that Jesus carried to Calvary. Yet, when my 'pied piper' played its tune, I followed it all the way into Jackie's arms.

By the time I was 18, I was regularly risking life and limb pursuing my one temptation in and out of bedrooms all over London. Every time a boyfriend or husband returned home unexpectedly, guess who was grinding his woman?

I used to think that nothing could come between me and my boy Andre, until he started rolling with Lorraine who made it clear to me, that she was not averse to a little slap and tickle on the side, and that no man had ever declined her sweet-honey-iced-tea (Boy, I didn't know that women possessed such deadly weapons of mass seduction).

Now the opportunity to bed a supermodel doesn't come every day, so what was I to do? My 'pied piper' didn't need three guesses before it started whistling that old refrain *tra-la-la-la-la-la-la-la-lee*... And before I knew it, I was savouring her mouth-watering sexual pleasures that Andre had confided in me so many times that he found irresistible. You see, Andre was always claiming that Lorraine had the sweetness to make a guy feel like his team have won the double but, when I checked it, that was just not the case. She was good, but my wide experience has taught me that the sweetest that a woman's sweetness gets is to make a guy feel like he's been to the movies. If there are any ladies out there who think that their sweetness is any better than that, please send me your phone numbers as I'd like a second opinion...

Only years later did I discover that, while I was studying the *Kama Sutra* with Lorraine, Andre was exchanging body fluids with my missus. Now that is what I call low...

At the end of the day, men are pathologically greedy when it comes to sex. It was Adam, not Eve who took a bite out of the apple. We, his descendants, can't resist a bite of the cherry, a bite of the peach and every other fruit available in the garden.

If only I could meet a woman without immediately thinking that I would do anything to bed her, I wouldn't be standing here naked, balancing myself precariously on a window ledge, twenty floors up in a Hackney high-rise.

SEX MACHINE OF THE WEEK

When you've done it all as a porn star, how do you rise to new challenges? For Hollywood porn supremo Jon Dough it had to be something a little bit out of the ordinary so he enlisted the help of 101 female helpers.

The idea was simple. He would set a new record for the most number of women bonked in a day by giving 'em all a good seeing to. The rules of engagement were fairly straight forward. Every women would receive at least five minutes of bonking and breaks in between would be supplemented by copious amounts of oral sex.

The session was quite a feat of endurance with Jon getting through bottles of water, sunblock and vaseline. Apparently the pain of using his privates all day was terrible and at the close of play he had tears rolling down his cheeks and his member was "an angry red colour you don't normally see outside of butchers' shops."

I've never won a Formula 1 race; set foot on the moon; caught the Loch Ness monster, or for that matter been invited to an orgy.

Whether I'll experience any of the aforementioned in my lifetime is debatable. The safe sex ethos of today means that at least one from this list seems as likely as Jamaica hosting the next Gay Olympics.

Now don't get me wrong, I can't say I'm desperate to be involved in an orgy (it's enough of an effort at times keeping one woman happy, never mind fourteen) but like the Queen's garden party, it would at least be nice to get an invite!

Somehow I doubt that the orgy scene is what it used to be. The social climate of today means that such hedonistic behaviour is probably only the pastime of a very small number.

I clocked the geezer with the 'I Love Orgies' T-shirt when on holiday in Mexico. Knowing Britain's reputation for producing cultural ambassadors, it wasn't surprising to discover that our man hailed from Oldham. He admitted that it was a very old T-shirt and that "Noor, mate. I ain't, like, ever been to orgy or nought. But I'm up fur a shag with any bird and her sister."

Aren't northern folk so quaint?

"Hey doc I've a problem, my son hasn't got a willy."

"But Sir, that's because it's a girl."

"Oh well in that case I'll take the receipt back and get the boy I ordered."

THE WOMAN'S POINT OF VIEW

Now the Bible I read says that God gave man 'dominion over the fish of the sea, and over the fowl of the air, and over the cattle, and over all the earth, and over every creeping thing that creepeth upon the earth', and that includes women. But no, herstorians won't have that. They claim that the original Bible (written in a language that only women can understand), states quite clearly that after God made man *she* told him in no uncertain terms, "Woman run t'ings." Why else would God have given man a willy if she didn't intend him to be a slave to his woman, they argue.

As far as *her*story is concerned, Jesus and the disciples were women, too. All except Judas, of course. Apparently, he was definitely a man.

With all this foolishness going around, is it any wonder that guys are insisting, once again, that women should stay home and do the cooking and

If all else fails...keep on denying it.

cleaning and, especially, the ironing?

History is a continuous, methodical record of man's achievements. *Her*story mentions man's 'achievement' in one sentence on page 233.

History shows that, since the beginning of time, the women who agree to 'love, honour and obey', get the full sweetness and never have to concern themselves about who else is sharing her coconut juice.

Take me and Sweetie for instance. When I told my very good bredrin, Patrick Augustus, that I was about to become a father for the first time, his immediate response was, "How do you know? Have you had a blood test yet?"

"But wait, Jah P, that is a completely reasonable and rational question," I rejoiced, touching fists with him. "I didn't think of that."

That's the good thing about guys, you can always count on your bredrin to give you good, sound, solid advice.

Sweetie didn't see it like that. I casually mentioned that a blood test might be in order, just so that we can both know for sure that the guilty sperm had my chromosomes in it. At the same moment as the suggestion left my lips, I felt a sharp sting in both

eyes. As Sweetie pulled her fingers out, she claimed that, coincidentally, I had something in each eye that she was trying to remove.

Yeah, *right!* They're called eyeballs, aren't they?

With tears streaming down my cheeks, I told Sweetie straight that, "Now I understand why so many guys have mistresses. I might even go out and find myself one..."

Ask me no questions, I'll tell you no lie. But whether it's true or not, I shouldn't have said it to Sweetie's face. At least not whilst standing within the same postal code area as she was in.

If women would put up with a lot more wotlessness, they'd have guys in abundance. Sweetie, however, seemed determined to separate my morals from my manhood.

"Baby, if you want me you're going to have to start obeying the Ten Commandments of Love.

I shouldn't have said that to Sweetie either, because the impact of the words caused the bottle of Guinness to accidently slip out of her hands and come whizzing past my ear at 85mph, exploding into the wall behind me.

My bonafide bredrin Patrick 'Original-Baby-Father-Catch-Me-If-You-Can' Augustus was the one

who first told me about the commandments:

1. Worship no other man but me.

2. Avoid all arguments. Tell me I'm right, even when I'm wrong.

3. Do not take my name in vain and run it all up and down town abusing me when you see me chirpsing a criss-looking woman on the street. Wait until we get home and we can discuss it calmly like civilized people, and you'll discover that the woman was probably my cousin...

4. Observe Sunday morning and keep it quiet. Do not jab me in the ribs and ask me where I think I've been all night, when I'm trying to get a full morning's sleep after a hectic night out raving. Skeen? Turn to Deutronomy 5 and you'll see quite clearly that, "the seventh day is a day of rest dedicated to ME!" *Skeen?*

5 Respect and honour me, so that all may go well with us and we may both live long...

6. Do not try to commit murder by slipping a little

'Oil of Keep-My-Man-Faithful' into the three meals a day you cook for me.

7. Don't even think about committing adultery... And, no, it's not the same thing when a man does.

8. Do not teef my filofax which is filled with the numbers of all my female cousins.

9. Do not accuse me falsely. Just because you catch me in bed with another woman, it does not necessarily mean that I have committed adultery. Like the saying goes, you have to catch me with both hands painted red before you can find me guilty.

10. Don't get gravilicious and covet the same Alfa Romeo convertible as your girlfriend, unless you can afford to pay for it and buy me one too.

"Tell Sweetie to learn the ten commandments and obey them," Patrick advised. "She's bond to see reason."

So I did.

In reply, she composed her own Ten Commandments of Love (from a Woman to a Man), and painted it across the bonnet of my Jag.

"That's what they call hormones," Patrick explained. "When a woman is pregnant, hormones make her see dirt inna your *yeye*, and makes bottles of Guinness slip out of her hands. Hormones make women do inexplicable things like paint your car with foolishness. It's happened to all of us when our partners have been pregnant. You've got to grin and bear it."

A FURTHER 12 FOR GOOD MEASURE

1. Baby, if you think you might be fat, you are. Don't ask, just get your big ass down to a gym.
2. Learn to work the toilet seat rather than complain. If it's up, put the rhatid t'ing down.
3. Don't change your hair. Ever.
4. If you ask a question you don't want an answer to, expect an answer you don't want to hear.
5. Sometimes I'm not thinking about you. Live with it.
6. Do not look upon shopping as a sport or artform.
7. Ask for what you want. Subtle hints don't work.
8. Say what you have to say during the commercials.
9. Check your oil. It is an essential part of the car.
10. A headache that lasts for seventeen months is a

problem. See a doctor.

11. Do not bring up anything said more than six months ago into an argument.

12. If you want some dessert after a meal, order some. You don't need to finish it. But please don't say, "No I couldn't/shouldn't/don't want any."

EROTIC FOOD FOR THOUGHT

Call me slim and shady, but I've always thought that 'girl' and 'power' were two words that went together like uncircumcised and rabbi. Yet to hear women talk about 'girl power' you would think that just because they are better educated, earn more money, are so high up the social ladder, have left the man so far behind in every respect, and now demand to be on top during intercourse, they therefore run t'ings, rule men, rule the world.

What a cheek!

Don't get me wrong, I'm all for women asserting themselves and playing football and becoming fighter pilots and getting drunk with the lads and joining us in the 'peeing for distance' competition afterwards, as long as they know their proper place at the side of man.

Behold the rib! A bone out of a man's side. If God

had meant for woman to have power and rule he would have taken that bone out of man's head. But no, he took a bone out of man's side, meaning that a woman must always stay at a man's side no matter what, even if he is wotless, unemployed and unfaithful. Ha! God knew what he was doing.

So much for girl power then. It came and fizzled out like a drunk man on his wedding night. Now things are nearly back to normal. Guys are once more lying on top and ladies are back to searching high and low for the longest, the leanest and the meanest.

Just rest yourselves, ladies. I'm not here to reaffirm the general superiority of men over women. God did not take that bone from our backsides, so he did not intend for men to sit on women, but if he had meant for you lot to have dominion over men, he would have given you balls. Stands to reason. Because real power is about who is able to dangle highly conspicuous and brightly coloured external genitals between his legs, screaming: "Look at me, I'm male."

Not that the possession of a large penis and clearly visible, loosely swinging pendulous testicles alone are sufficient to bestow power willy (oops) nilly. But with so many women complaining that they have climbed so high up the social ladder while leaving your average man so far behind that they can hardly find one to match them, it seems that the handful of us who are on their level (intelligent, successful, upwardly mobile, courteous, speak proper and smell nice) have a lot more power than we deserve. Take me for instance, I'm not even that good looking, but you want to check some of the pretty hot and tempting babes willing to do all kinds of freaky stuff on my behalf. Now, that's what I call power.

Back in the day when women were were in short supply and it was men who were in abundance, it was you lot who had all the power. Take Helen of Troy, her power was so great that men killed each other over her. Cleopatra, too. You don't get that nowadays. Women kill each other over men, yes, you can see that every saturday afternoon at your local supermarket. But guys nowadays aren't too bothered if their woman gets ignorant, because they can go out and get another one, just like that.

Or at least that's what I thought when Ms XXXXXX came up to me at a recent buppie event at a top West End hotel and whispered "Superpussy?" in my ear. I should have said "I'll have the soup," but guys being what they are, I found myself exercising my power prerogative and allowing her to drive me home to her posh semi in Temple Fortune for a night of unrestrained passion.

I thought nothing of it when she pulled out the handcuffs, I was game if she was game.

I've been chained to the bed for five days. I haven't had a taste of soup or anything else. All I get is Ms XXXXX telling me this same story over and over:

"When God made man and all the different parts of the body were fighting over who should be boss. Apparently the brain demanded the position because it was the cleverest. The arms and legs said they should be boss because they were the strongest. The stomach said it should, because it took in all the nutrition and fed man. Then the anus said it should be boss... The others laughed out loud and said, 'You, but you're just an asshole.'

The anus got vexed and locked itself tight. After a few days, man started getting dizzy. After a few weeks he couldn't move at all and the body shut down. The other parts of the body had to concede that power resides even in assholes."

BABY FATHERS ARE NOT JUST FOR XMAS

Talking of fathers, ladies, thank God for the father of your child. Yes, we may be wotless, ignorant, irresponsible and unable to control our libidos, but without us there would be no little bundle of joy. So, ladies, Christmas is as good a time as any to get down on your knees and thank God for man's seed.

Unfortunately, due to certain circumstances beyond our control, not every father is able to spend and enjoy Christmas with any and every one of his pickneys dem. I'm speaking, of course, about that figure of fun and jocularity in the community, the serial baby father... Britain's Most Wanted. Spare a thought this Christmas for this poor creature, to whom December 25th is like a stock market crash.

My poor friend Johnny PickneyDaddy (not his real name), for example, has to pawn his car every Christmas just to juggle his head above water. 'Cause he's got 67 christmas cards to buy and 67 Play

Stations, too. Unfortunately for him, he has trouble remembering each one of his children's names, even though most of the boys are called Junior. He also has trouble remembering where they all live. Because he's been on the run, so to speak. Particularly since a posse of baby mothers' mothers informed him, in no uncertain terms, of what they would do to him with a meat cleaver should they catch hold of him.

Thankfully for him, the CSA have all the addresses to his 67 children, and his baby mothers' paying-in account numbers, too.

To save himself having to write out Christmas messages over and over again, PickneyDaddy recently composed the following 'universal xmas letter from a baby father' which he has photocopied 67 times:

*Dear*_____ *(please fill in yourself)*

How are you? Merry Xmas. Hope you liked the Action Man I bought you last Xmas.

How is school? How are you? Do you know who I am? What do you want to be when you grow up?

How are you? Sorry I can't make it this Xmas. Hope you like the Play Station. Be good, and if you can't be good be careful. *From your Uncle Johnny*

Let's call a truce this year, ladies. Let bygones be bygones. Let baby mother and baby father come together in one love and unity this Christmas. Even if Pappa's got to hit and run, bite your tongue and try to maintain a friendly smile. Even when he says, "See you next Christmas", keep at arm's length away from that meat cleaver. The Accident and Emergency wards are too full already every Christmas with guys missing some essential part of their anatomy simply because of some careless remark during the Queen's speech. Please, ladies, positively NO slackness this Christmas.

And if you've got a man of your own this Christmas, then bully for you, and thank God for that too. Even if he is unable (due to circumstances beyond his control), to actually be by your side on the day. Let's face it, it's going to be homely for some this Christmas and lonely for others. It's a fact of life beyond refutation. I, personally, wish it wasn't. But seeing it's got to be that way, my wish this Christmas would be that all parties approached this in a civilized way with the wives and sweethearts coming together and agreeing to share their man for the twenty-four hour duration (this is, after all, the season of goodwill to all), which would get me out of

"I can always tell when it's Christmas. It's the only time I see you with your child."

the predicament of how I'm supposed to be in east London, west London and south London all at the same time.

And if you haven't got a man this Christmas, then thank God for that too because without Him (or Her) there would have been no immaculate conception and hence no office xmas parties, that annual excuse to get off your head and into bed with your boss in the hope that you'll be included in his/her New Year's Promotion List. It may come as a blow to you, but take a good look at that colleague of yours who seems determined to make sure the party ends with a bang, s/he could be your next head of department with the power to hire and fire.

MEN ARE DOGS, WOMEN ARE BITCHES

Both take up too much space on the bed.

Both have irrational fears about vacuum cleaning.

Both are threatened by their own kind.

Both like to chew wood.

Both mark their territory.

Both are bad at asking questions.

Neither says what's bothering them.

Both tend to smell riper with age.

The smaller ones tend to be more nervous.

Neither do dishes.

Both fart shamelessly.

Both like dominance games.

You've a woman who's just gone out on a date with this nice guy you met at the supermarket. What is the question your girlfriends are all gonna ask you? Oh yes, that time honoured favourite of, "What does he do for a living?" Or to cut to the bottom line. How

"Leave me alone woman. I'll hug you after the world cup."

much wonga does he earn, and is he worth dropping the panties for?

It don't matter how ugly that sucker is, how bad his breath or dress sense is, he can have the social graces of Godzilla and the brains of a not too clever house plant. But let my man be rolling in the spondoolies and I can bet your big ass that Mr Fright will be pulling more crackers than the whole town on Christmas Day.

Every guy has looked at a criss gal on the arms of something that was at the bottom rung of Darwin's evolution chart, and wondered to himself, 'What has he got that I ain't got'? Five noughts after the first digit of his salary cheque, dummy. That's what he's got.

So you think I'm exaggerating? Well how the hell do you think someone as ugly as...*(please fill in)*... could ever get a babe? When he fell out of the ugly tree, that sucker hit every god damn branch! Even someone that ugly must own a mirror in their yard.

Check out the findings of a recent survey conducted by researchers at University College of Los Angeles (UCLA). The survey of 3,407 single men and women aged between 18 to 55, revealed that for women, a man's income potential was more important than his physical attractiveness, education or occupation.

These academics need to seriously question where they keep their brains. These jerk-offs wasted god knows how much time and dollars interviewing thousands of people to come up with results I could have told them for nothing! One phone call is all it would have taken, but no, they've got to go and discover the blindingly obvious for themselves.

Ever since the first man built up a fine collection of sabre-tooth tiger skins and realised that as a result he had his pick of the nicest cave women, guys have known the score. The more the dunza you hold the bigger the choice when it comes to the ladies.

In turn, women knew that all they had to do to pull Mr Right was to look good and dress nice. Indeed the UCLA survey found that men place most emphasis on physical beauty when it comes to choosing a partner than on anything else. Guy's just ain't too deep, I'm afraid. Good chest, nice ass, pretty face is the sophisticated criteria most guys use in the selection process.

However, women be warned. The times they are a-changing! Going back again to this UCLA survey, the only important factor that the researchers found was that a growing number of men are going out with a woman because of how much money she earns. The study shows that men are now placing a potential wife's income as more important than her age, race or religion.

"We might expect women to consider a man's earning potential but not men," explains UCLA psychologist Belinda Tucker. "This reflects the new reality for men. Making it today often requires two income-producing partners."

I think Ms Tucker has hit the nail squarely on its head. A few years back many guys I knew just checked a woman for her crissness, now many of these same fellas ain't into a nice ass but more concerned with a woman's assets. The reality is that as time goes by even the most hardened playa starts to realise that gal fitness ain't gonna pay the mortgage. What job your potential missus does is going to determine what kind of lifestyle you're going to have together.

However, things ain't always that rosy in the garden. I recently saw my spar go gaga for a woman who I thought wasn't right for him. He just met the gal and was already booking the church for the big day. Then disaster struck. He found he couldn't get on with her. He had got so caught up in fantasising about the suburban dream home that their joint incomes could buy as a married couple that he became blind to the reality.

But he ain't the only guy just looking at the dollars. A woman friend of mine has just blown her savings on a seriously wicked-looking Beemer convertible. The reaction from guys has been crazy, she says. Men are now coming up to her and asking her out all the time because they think she is in some well paid high-flying job.

As I said, the times they are a-changing. Man is no longer the hunter and the provider while the good woman stays at home and skins the dead woolly mammoth. The roles of provider are now being more evenly split between man and woman. At the end of the day that must be a good thing. One day maybe a woman may even take me out for dinner and actually pay for the meal!

But whatsoever the cause is, one may say, that there are months which women grow more merry in...

That's why you'll rarely see a guy with his own woman at carnival. You'll see him with somebody else's woman, but more often than not you'll see him looking cool, detached and single with a Dragon stout in his hand, ready and willing to offer his services to a world-a-girls, no questions asked. Many of you will have seen me there already.

It is, however, worrying for us thirtysomething guys to know that the x-rated carnival theme once again this year is 'Toyboys', the current in-thing amongst women who are old enough to be their mothers.

As a man of considerable and reputed high moral standing, I find this penchant for younger men, frankly, quite obscene. There should be a law against it. That these younger boys are like a Duracell, keep going a lot longer than thirtysomething guys like myself, is a point of issue on which I will not vent my anger for the moment.

Show me a woman who dates younger men, and I'll show you a woman who has considered homicide when her partner left her for a younger woman.

Take Sweetie, who is threatening to trade me in for two boys of twenty. "Birds do it, bees do it, men do it, even educated fleas do it, so what's wrong with me doing it?" she asked innocently.

That's not how it works, ladies, the natural order of things don't go that way. Read Charles Darwin's

"Let me clarify one point. I actually said 'I sacked the President's cook'"

Origins of the Species and you'll see that it's not DO AS MEN DO, it's DO AS YOU'RE SUPPOSED TO DO. Like the sun's not supposed to rise in the west and set in the east, like men ain't supposed to wear dresses, women are not supposed to have partners who are younger than they are. The very thought of it is an abomination.

Ladies, take a totally objective tip from me. Younger guys can't do nothing for you but make you wish that you were with a more mature man like myself. It takes more than youth to satisfy a REAL woman. Trust me, I should know, I know women better than they know themselves. Besides, I used to be a toyboy myself, and I can honestly say that I didn't have a clue what I was doing until I was, oh, at least thirty. Now though, I'm an expert in the art of female seduction and always provide a five-year guarantee of satisfaction (or your sweet honey back) to any woman I meet at carnival (now, tell me ladies, which snotty nosed youth can give you that?)

And when it comes to stamina, guys my age can now match the reggae boyz grind for grind, thanks to the new wonder drug Viagara which keeps it up longer and stronger and puts the spunk back into balls and chains without 'no pain no gain'. I've only taken one dose and already I feel twenty years younger. In fact I feel like a gal who is twenty years younger.

Ladies, you're just going to have to accept the fact that it's an unequal world. Guys can get away with things that you will never be able to get away with, not until the sun rises in the west and sets in the east.

IT'S A MAN *THANG*, YOU WOULDN'T UNDERSTAND

There are only half a dozen sensitive men out there and, frankly, I ain't one of them. In fact, there's nothing I find more distasteful than seeing a grown up man unable to control his emotion in public. Guys like that give the rest of us a bad name. I'm the Original Man — hard as nails, tough as leather, the stain that Ajax cannot remove. Ya get me?

Sweetie, however, is determined to reduce me to a blubbering blubber of sensitivity even if it means tying a team of eight horses to my balls and cracking a whip across their backs.

In her efforts to conjure up my sensitive side, she has recently taken to blackmailing me: I'LL cook — YOU'LL eat — WE'LL go to the ballet/opera/ rent a black and white 'weepie' from the video store and wrap up comfy together at home with a hot cup of

Cadbury's Options and a box of Ferrero Rochero chocolates.

"After all," she reasoned, "we're having a child together, if you don't show your emotions, how am I supposed to know what's on your mind?"

EXACTLY.

Sweetie wouldn't want to know what was on my mind at this precise moment. How could I tell her that I knew damn well she didn't have a baby in her belly? That I have total faith in my French friend, Rex du Fétherlite, and that I was only humoring her by agreeing to accompany her for a scan at the hospital? I live and die by the Original Man motto: *If the milk ain't spilt, then don't cry over it.* You see, ladies, the reason guys don't show their emotions is because we don't want to upset y'all. *That's* how sensitive we are!

So I put on some darkers and wore the afro wig that I had been saving for the 'I'm black and I'm proud — SAY IT LOUD!' '70s revival that has still not happened, and followed her to the hospital, low profile of course 'cause the last place a high profile playa like myself wants to be recognised is at the maternity ward.

The New Age Man says: "Me and my partner will share the birth experience. I will be there in the labour ward and hold her hand throughout as our baby pops out covered in slime, 'cause that's the kind of dude I am." The Original Man, on the other hand, says: "Guys got no business in maternity wards unless they're planning on getting pregnant (or they've got a loaded gun shoved up their bum)."

It's true, there is a worldwide conspiracy against me. And Dr Popodopolous is part of that conspiracy.

I followed Sweetie into the ultrasound room humming 'Billie Jean' (But the kid is not my own...) Dr Popodopolous took one look at me and asked Sweetie if I was the father. She nodded. I shrugged my shoulders and answered, "Innocent 'til proven."

The doctor turned to Sweetie and said, "Make sure he does ALL the work for you from now on... You have to rest, he has to do ALL the shopping and ALL the cleaning and wait on you hand and foot...."

Yeah, *right!* Thanks a lot, Doc.

I looked at my watch. I had been there five minutes already. I told the Doc to step up a gear — I had things to do, places to go, people to see...

Yes, there's definitely a conspiracy against the Original Man and it seems like God is now part of that conspiracy too, because up on the monitor beside Dr Popodopolous was a scan of Sweetie's belly and there, for all the world to see spinning around in a sea of amniotic fluid, was a miniature Dotun waving at me as if to say, "See ya in a couple of months, and oh... by the way, I'm going to be a handful."

I can't explain the next thing that happened to me. Call it wotlessness or foolishness or cry out "SHAME!" As I said, the Original Man won't cry you a river. But there was something about the way the baby held his hand, exactly the way I hold mine, that told me straight away that, yep, the milk was definitely spilt and, despite myself, I started bawling like a new born baby.

It was embarrassing. I couldn't stop myself. I bawled so loud that doctors and nurses rushed in from other wards to see what the commotion was all about. Finally Sweetie had to slap me hard after telling me "enough's enough" a dozen times.

Still today, whenever I look at that scanned photo of my little baby, it's the same reaction. The neighbours have to close their windows and draw their curtains as the sound of the Original Man bawling carries all the way down the street.

The question is, why am I crying? Is it joy or is it pain at not being able to afford a one-way ticket to Rio just when I need it most.

PLAYA NO MORE

Don't wanna be a playa no more. Because I've been around the world and played the field long enough. Now I'm ready to settle down and go legit with a partner for life — finally.

Don't wanna be a playa no more. I've got so much love inside me, it's bursting to get out.

Don't wanna be a playa no more, but that's easier said than done. Despite my impeccable credentials and my Mr Ibiza 1989 runners-up title, I can't seem to convince the women I'm interested in to consider me as anything more than an occasional bonk, while those that are interested are not quite what I was looking for.

You see, when it comes to finding a man to spend the rest of their life with, too many women nowadays are looking to settle down with an American Express platinum card. They'll 'settle' for nothing less.

Women like that say they're looking for love, when

"Baby, I'm still not sure this style suits me."

they're better off reading a romance novel.

"Don't wanna be a playa no more," I told Patrick, and he suggested that I place an ad on the lonely hearts line:

Sincere and Sensitive SBM (no kids yet), 37, WLTM SBF 18-35 for TLC and more. NTW.

A few days later, I got half a dozen messages on my personal voice box. Shereen sounded the sweetest, so I called her up first. She answered with a voice that sounded less cultured than I remembered it and which had lost its sweetness.

The first thing she said was, "How tall are you?" It wasn't a question, but a threat. Then she wanted to know how much I earned, whether I was fat, how many times a week I went down to the gym and whether I was average or above average good looking. Finally, she wanted to know where I got that funny name from. "I hope you're not African," she warned.

What could I say?

"I am out of your league," she informed me, "set your sights lower next time."

Click.

I rang Beverly and got her 'call waiting'. "My sister's on the other line," she said, when she finally answered. "Give me a moment and I'll get rid of her."

I waited on the line for half a minute until her return.

Beverly had previously left a message on my personal voice box saying that I sounded really interesting. When she now came on the line, we chatted for about an hour, she sounded really interesting, too. We arranged to meet up. I put down the phone. A few moments later Beverly called back and immediately started apologising and saying that she'd been speaking to her sister for the last hour. I explained that she had got me mixed up with some other man, that I was the one who she had been on the phone to. That was when she recognised my voice and put down the phone hurriedly. I hadn't realised that she was a 'serial date' who spent her time scanning the lonely hearts line for every available man. Her inadvertent admission that she bought condoms and K-Y Jelly by the truckload should have warned me off.

Needless to say, I didn't go on that date.

Next was Denise. But she failed my '20 Question Rule' (I asked her 20 questions about herself before she asked me one about myself.)

I did go out with Angie, though, for an enjoyable and romantic dinner for two in Camden Town. Though her failure to reach for her purse even in a feigned attempt to 'go dutch' displayed a stunning ignorance of basic economics, by the end of the evening, I could feel that tell-tale sign in my loins (it's a man *thang* — you wouldn't understand it) which kept telling me that this could really be THE ONE. But then she discovered that I was a Virgo and that was it, I was history. There was no remote chance of a quick one back at her place or mine afterwards, either. "That just wouldn't do," she insisted. "I'm a Libra. Earth signs and air signs don't mix..."

Don't wanna be a playa no more, so I called up the lonely hearts line again and put in another ad:

Hey good lookin'!
(Extremely) handsome SBM, 30ish, high rollin' with own successful company and penthouse. Slick, well-toned body and drives Jag, but still a lonely lover.
WLTM naughty but nice SBF, 18-35, for good times and jetsetting. Sweetness guaranteed!

There were over eighty messages on my voice box. I even got a message from that same Shereen, who mentioned what a beautiful 'roots' name I had, and said how much she loved African guys.

Click.

Of the other seventy-nine, I dated two women. Laverne, was a thirty-three-year-old civil servant with the Home Office in Croydon, and lived in Thornton Heath with her eight-year-old son. I took her to the theatre. I had a great time. Laverne, on the other hand, sat with a sour look on her face, mumbling something about how my body looked less slick and well-toned than she had imagined! As if that wasn't bad enough, when I took her back to my 'penthouse' on the top floor of my council block, she started cussing bad word for the entire neighbourhood to hear. Talk about SHAME! Her repeated comments such as, "Is it still called a penis when it's that small?" were both uncalled for and thoughtless. Moreover, although her inability to achieve orgasm was of paramount importance to me, her suggestion that we invite three of my mates to join us and help me out, seemed somewhat extreme and inappropriate.

But then I dated Jackie O and I forgot all about shame. Instead I was thanking God that you really could find the perfect partner through heart to hearts.

27-year-old Jackie O(swald) looks so good, that for a moment I didn't care whether she was able to string two sentences together or not. Sump'n could really gwan here, I was thinking.

However, Jackie could do more than string a few

sentences together. We met at the Spot in Covent Garden and, in between drinks, that first hour was one long monologue by Jackie O. You see, Jackie liked to talk — about herself. And she had to be all EXTRA about it: "D'you like my hair? It cost me eighty pounds, you know. Oh, I won't let anyone but Silvio do it, he used to do Lady Di's... Spike Lee's promised to give me a part in his next film... I was at Lennox Lewis' birthday party in Ascot... So many men want to marry me at the moment, you wouldn't believe it...I only do the dateline for a laugh really."

Several drinks later, I was so bored I told her I was too drunk to drive her home and gave her a tenner for a taxi before beating a hasty retreat to spend yet another lonely night, in bed, with only my giant teddy to cuddle up to.

Don't wanna be a playa no more. So if it's dreams that you want, I can sell you dreams. I've hired a Mercedes convertible for the weekend, I've booked tickets on Eurostar and I'm currently adjusting some figures to qualify for that platinum card.

Maybe I'll be able to stop being a playa soon. Who knows? It depends on whether women have stopped making unrealistic demands on us sensitive guys...

HE LOVES ME, HE LOVES ME NOT...

Just because my idea of fun on Valentine's Day is sending Buju Banton a card 'from a tall, dark and very butch admirer with a big, thick, black moustache', malicious gossipers will have you believe that men are not very romantic. If truth be known, we would like nothing more than to see our partners get their minimum daily requirement of romance 365 days a year, but women are giving it up so easily nowadays that there hardly seems much point in wooing.

He loves me, he loves me not. He loves me...

So who let the dogs out? Back in the day when romance was a man's sneaky way of getting sex, you couldn't stop us buying flowers daily, taking our women to fancy restaurants weekly, and whisking them away for a romantic weekend for two in a country hotel every month to cherish each other's uniqueness and celebrate our lives together.

Remember when? Nowadays some men have hardly spent change in a bar before they've pulled. I know guys have their faults, but we are easier to train than dogs.

He loves me, he loves me not. He loves me...

Three cheers then for St Valentine's Day when we've got to put a bit more effort into it — set the mood, play the music, dress the part, say the right words, do the little things; when we get to put a bit more imagination into romance; when we get to cook dinner then cover our partner's body with it and then get to lick it off, read lingerie catalogues and buy boxes of erotic chocolate (with milk chocolate breasts and dark chocolate nipples) without anyone thinking that you're a pervert. For, as every man knows, the sugar always tastes sweetest after you've had to invest in a round the world cruise with a week's indulgence at the Sandy Lane Hotel in Barbados where a Rolls Royce picks you up at the airport, champagne accompanies nearly everything and where every room comes with its own private valet.

He loves me, he loves me not. He loves me...

Ladies, the Day of Reckoning is once again upon us, and the Moment of Truth beckons. You can run, but there will be no hiding place from St. Valentine's

Day, 'cause that's when you get to find out irrefutably whether your man cares for his 'outside woman' more than he cares for you.

He loves me, he loves me not. He loves me...?

That is the BIG question on Valentine's Day, but you don't have to dismember a flower petal by petal to find out. Those days are long gone, as are the days of finding satisfaction in a cheap card with a vintage cliché: 'Roses are red, violets are blue/Licorice is yummy, and black like you.' Let's face it, if a man can't spend the whole of Valentine's with his woman when it falls on a weekend, he's got to be tickling someone else's erogenous zones.

He loves me, he loves me not. He loves me...

You've been dying to find out for sure because, like Thomas, you women are very unbelieving (which is just as well, for guys are extremely deceiving). If you're a true blue woman, you may have your suspicions already, and are just biding your time cleaning the meat cleaver in readiness for the St. Valentine's Day massacre. But more than likely, your man is a real-deal undercover lover playa and you haven't got a clue. Why, as you're reading this you're probably thinking, 'I KNOW my man ain't like that.' Yeah, *right*. Remember, it only takes an

HOW TO BUILD YOUR OWN LUNCH BOX

Sick of having a rice grain for a dick? Tired of gyal mistaking your dick for a pubic hair. Well your prayers have been answered. You no-longer have to hold your sausage hostage. Now is the chance to be the packed mac-daddy that you have always wanted to be with *BMW*'s own guide to being the proud owner of your own organic King-sized snicker Bar.

STAGE 1

INSTRUCTIONS:

STAGE 1: First go to the shop and buy one pair of denier tights (colour is optional). Get an old 'lengthy shoe lace and tie both ends to the end of the tight.

STAGE 2: Then go to a building sites and teef one of them safety helmets and stuff the helmet to the end of the tights.

STAGE 2

BLACK HISTORY 14: THE REAL REASON WHY ENGLAN' WON THE WORLD CUP IN 1966.

hour and forty five minutes of non-stop bumping and grinding to be unfaithful. You still refuse to believe me? Well, church bells sometimes do better work than the sermon, so while you're watching the omnibus edition of *Eastenders* alone on the 14th, consider whether that ringing in your ears isn't actually your man moaning and groaning in someone else's bed.

He loves me, he loves me not. He loves me...

Sadly, the anticipation of St Valentine's Day is usually more exciting than the day itself. For the 364 days prior, you have looked forward to this one day of oneness and exchanged vows with your main squeeze. You've planned for it and prepared for it with an intensive programme of aerobics, because you know that this is the one day when there will be no flim flam and no excuses. Then you get a call saying he's broken down on the motorway miles from anywhere...

He loves me, he loves me not. He loves me...?

As it is mathematically impossible for a guy to spend Valentine's night with two sweethearts in different places at the same time, it is safe to deduce that if he's not spending the whole of Valentine's with you, he's spending it with somebody else.

Elementary, my dear. You see, all lies die when the truth is told.

He loves me, he loves me not. He loves me...

He probably doesn't, if on the 14th he hasn't brought you breakfast in bed, butt naked except for that full-length mink coat you've always wanted, offering a gentle massage of your foot bottom as you nibble on a *petit beurre* (not to talk of filling the bedroom with hundreds of helium balloons with a romantic message tied to each one). If he really loved you, the words 'I love you' would be carved into the Haagen Dazs ice cream he's brought you for breakfast and, on the tray beside it, the book *Sensual Oral Lovemaking: A Beginner's Guide*, would wink at you and smile, with two tickets for that round-the-world cruise on the QE2 tucked inside. Yes, if he really loved you, you wouldn't have to spend Sunday the 14th sitting by the radio listening out for his dedication while he's out doing his 'runnings'. Life is too short and too full of blisters for you to be hanging around all Valentine's Day waiting for him to pop the question, or to end up having to pop *him* for not popping *it*. You see, if he really *really* loves you, there'll be an engagement ring at the bottom of that tub of ice cream. Let's be honest, if he really, really,

really loves you, he would treat you to a one hour, no limit shopping spree in your favourite mall this Valentine's. If you want to find out whether your man gives tuppence for your love, distress his credit cards on the 14th and see if he flinches.

Faced with another 'licensed to pay bills' day so soon after Christmas, most guys will plead poverty. This lame excuse translates loosely as, 'Darling, I can't afford to pay for you *and* my sweetheart.' Fair enough. If money's too tight to mention and his budget won't stretch to two, the least he could do this Valentine's is book the cheapest room in an expensive hotel for the two of you and take you to an expensive restaurant where you only order an aperitif. However, if your man's one ah dem bruddahs who has sewn together the corners of his wallet, he could still prove he loves you by leaving 365 messages on your answering machine saying simply *'Voulez-vous couchez avec moi, ce soir'*; or by taking you back to the place where you first met and spending the day together simply holding hands and reminiscing; by liberating a street sign with your name on it and wrapping it up nicely before presenting it to you. The very, *very* least he could do is buy you a box of Roses and spend Valentine's Day getting fat with you.

"Listen Shanise, when I said to use a flower to play 'he loves me, he loves me not' that ain't what I meant at all."

He loves you not....

If you t'ink a lie me ah tell, then ask Busty Bridget an' Big Batty Patty, too. Their motto is: 'If he ain't spending every night with you, he's spending it with somebody else. Because every man should be with the woman he loves on Valentine's, and Valentine's is twenty-four sevens, three sixty-five. She who does not heed these words will feel it.'

Maybe I will, Maybe I won't...

The time eventually comes when every guy has to invest at least £16.29 (Argos prices) in a ring and get down on one knee and make a fool of himself in public, just because it's February 14th. Yet, year after year we 'forget' to book that table for two at a romantic restaurant, in order to put off JUDGEMENT DAY a little longer. This year, however, Sweetie's gone and invested in a restaurant! She says we'll always have a table for two there, even when it's fully booked. Now, I just can't figure out how I'm going to make sure that ST. VALENTINE'S DAY AIN'T VALENTINE'S DAY.

Maybe I will, maybe I won't...
Maybe I will, maybe I won't...
Maybe I will, maybe I won't.

What could possibly possess the ultimate Mr.

Lover-Lover to even CONTEMPLATE the 'M' word, I hear you ask. It must be a financial t'ing. Crafty old Dotun, I hear you say, Sweetie must have money like Ivana Trump. Why else would Mr. Lover-Lover give up all those good times, all that independence and freedom? Or maybe he's gone all soft. He even wrote Sweetie a sonnet, you know. It read:

Shall I compare thee to my Benz or my Beemer?

A Lexus is far more grand, but your waist is much trimmer.

Maybe I will, maybe I won't... My heart says 'do the right t'ing', but my bonafide bredrin are counting on me to do no such thing. Patrick warned me:

"It's a decision that you'll regret for the rest of your life. It means no more getting off with the EXCESS amount of CRISS women out there, no more new romances, no more raving all night and hangin' out with the homies (but especially no more getting off with the EXCESS amount of women). You will never be allowed to go ANYWHERE ever again and you will have to live with the same woman for the rest of your life...!!! Walking down the aisle is like walking the plank. Marriage is a life sentence with hard labour. And, anyway, if God had meant guys to be married, he would have created women who knew how to love, honour and, especially, OBEY! If a marriage licence was like a driver's licence that expired every few years I'd say, fine, but marriage isn't just for Christmas, you know, it's for life. Don't make the same mistake we made, I beg yuh..."

Maybe I will, maybe I won't. Maybe I WILL..:

Trevor encouraged me:

"It's about time we built a solid foundation for the family instead of having children all over the place. And marriage is the best thing you can do. It's a challenge, not for weakhearts. It's a lot of hard work, but the pay-off is unimaginable bliss. Especially if you marry a woman. Your whole life will be transformed for the better. But then again, most men are never going to realise that... which is okay, because there are plenty of women who will..."

Maybe I will, maybe I won't... Maybe I will...

Maybe I WON'T when I think of all the miserable husbands I meet every day, looking like they've got a permanent shotgun up their ample behinds (coaxed by good ol' 'married-life cooking' to spread a couple more inches every week since they first popped the question, making them — coincidentally, I'm sure, ladies — totally unattractive to the female species). I WON'T if I take a moment to find ten thousand good reasons why I shouldn't, or if I consider what

Socrates would have said if he was in the same position: "If you don't get married, you won't regret getting married..."

Maybe I will, maybe I won't...

Maybe I WILL when I think of all the good times we could have together and how my standard of living could go up dramatically when we put our joint incomes together. Together, we could get that big house in a nice neighbourhood. Together we could afford to go on three holidays every year. Change our car every two years. We could be rich together! I WILL if Sweetie wins the lottery by SAINT VALENTINE'S DAY or if I get very drunk.

Maybe I WILL if I think about how crazy I am about Sweetie. But, then again, what's love got to do with it?

THE TROUBLE WITH MEN

It's a troubled world and it's one that is changing at
an amazing rate. The trouble is that men ain't
changing quickly enough to keep up. My spar
Lincoln, can't change and he won't change. That's
where his trouble lies.

Lincoln seemingly has it all. He earns good corn as
a qualified accountant and has the nice house, car etc,
etc. But he can never hold on to the similar
lifestyle/career women that he starts relationships
with. Things tend to last for a few months then the
woman chips. The trouble is obvious to the most
casual observer, but not to Lincoln.

You see, my man, nice as he is, hasn't realised that
the world has moved on a few thousand years.
Lincoln still believes that Tyrannosorous Rex roams
the wild open plains of Europe and that fire comes
from rubbing two sticks together. Lincoln is the
proverbial caveman, the sort of guy who thinks the

word 'macho' is effeminate.

If you want to be a caveman that's your choice, but as Lincoln has discovered, women who've got it going on just ain't gonna put up with living in a cave and being dragged there by their weave to cook some dinosaur steak over an open fire.

I've tried to explain how t'ings run these days to him, but he just doesn't get it. When the last woman left him he asked me where he'd gone wrong. "Try using some SENSITIVITY," I advised. "Sensitivity?" He asked puzzled. "I don't really check for them fancy kinds of aftershave."

Lincoln is vexed because the last woman is now going out with a white guy and he's on that white guy/black woman trip. He just can't see that times have moved on and that sistas ain't gonna be putting up with the macho foolishness anymore.

My friend Angela is I think typical of many black women today. She says she would like to settle down with a brotha but says she thinks it likely she'll end up with a white guy. The reason? "Because the white guys I've been out with have treated me so much better. They have been sensitive, supportive, committed and have respected me more." When you ask the same question to half a dozen other black women and you get the same answer, then you have to seriously start wondering.

Black men's biggest problem is this one of playing Mr Macho. It's particularly the case with Caribbean men, and most so the case with Jamaican male culture. You've gotta play it tough and cool with the right amount of attitude at all times. Any emotions (except anger) that you show are seen as a sign of weakness. If you speak too articulatedly you're talking like a 'white man'. If you're concerned about the feelings of others you're 'soft'. And if you help your women around the house you're a 'maama man'.

Rationally, men can sit down and laugh about black male machoness, but it's surprising how deep the cultural conditioning goes. In so many situations you find yourself trying to rationalise your attitude but go ahead and be Mr Ignorant all the same. If you've been brought up with certain attitudes it ain't always easy to leave them behind.

As we know the world moves on.My advise to Lincoln and similar brothas everywhere is to check yourself or be left behind. T'ings ain't easy when you're the last caveman in town.

5 REASONS TO TAKE COVER WHEN A COCK'S ABOUT (MORE CAVEMAN BUSINESS)

1. It is defective. It has a hole in it.

2. It has poor character.

3. It hangs out with a couple of nuts.

4. It lives next to an asshole.

5. It is subject to anxiety attacks (when it gets excited it throws up and faints).

'When you've got to go, you've got to go' is how the expression runs but it seems that many guys have interpreted the expression as to read 'When you've got to come'...

I was given reason to reflect upon this almost Zen-like philosophy last week on the number 65 bus in Richmond. I happened to gaze out of the bus window and to my disgust saw Mr Suburban in his Vauxhall Frontera having a five finger shuffle on his pee pump. (I would have used the word 'wank' but I don't want to offend anybody!)

The incident confirmed what I've always said of Frontera owners, but I really didn't expect to see someone taking my description quite so literally.

Thankfully he shot off before he got any further. Let me rephrase that. He drove off very quickly down the road before the top deck had to witness any further developments.

I don't know about the rest of you lot, but I can't say that driving around in London's bumper-to-bumper traffic puts me in anything resembling an aroused state. It therefore makes me seriously wonder what kind of geezer feels the urge to pull his plonker while going about his business.

I mean how does it go so? Do you suddenly find yourself bored with the car's radio that you think 'oh I might as well have a wank? Is life so busy these days that you can't find a few minutes before bedtime to get out the box of Kleenex and check the pile of mags under the mattress? Does driving a 4X4 vehicle bring out the worst in people? I just don't get it.

But matey ain't alone in picking the most public of places to play with his privates. My spar's brother is a copper and he tells me that they come across people having a hand shandy in the strangest of places. Apparently a favourite in suburbia is the midnight call where the geezer next door likes nothing better that to go into his neighbour's garden and have a crafty pull. It's often assumed by an eagle-eyed, nosey neighbour that it's a burglar and call up the old bill.

They even caught one guy having a pull over a Rolls Royce parked in an NCP car park. Mr Copper reckons that it's all kinds of people at it and not just the dirty old raincoat brigade. He has one interesting observation, namely that he has never caught a woman doing the equivalent. I'm not surprised, women don't have a dong and therefore are not prone to some of the illogical acts that some geezers get up to.

An ex-girlfriend always used to love telling me some of the sad things guys got up to when it came to solitary pleasures. As a former hospital nurse she saw some of the unfortunate consequences of an over-active sex drive and a fascination with inanimate objects. For example, she was on duty at the emergency and casualty department one night when some geezer arrived with a ring spanner stuck fast around his member.

Not being satisfied with using his hand like normal people, Mr Wannabe mechanic had decided to use a spanner. He was in some pain and panic so girlfriend thought it would be funny to tell him that they would have to amputate his dong. "The guy nearly fainted," she told me with glee. Fortunately for him some ice water and vaseline did the trick.

If this story doesn't serve as a warning to any guy thinking of trying something different tonight, then nothing will. But the crux of the matter is that some geezers are so set on having a pull whatever the place or circumstances, that nothing is gonna stop them going for it.

To any Frontera owners reading this, please be aware of the possible implications of being near a double decker bus before you reach for the woodpecker.

To be or not to be single, that is the burning question that many guys wrestle with daily. For women, it's straightforward: you're either single or you're not. But for guys the problem is much more complex. For example, we see no contradiction in holding two seemingly diametrically opposing positions on the matter. For guys it is quite feasible to be having a relationship and to still be single. Why, I even know some guys who are married with kids, yet maintain that they are young, free and single (especially when the enquiry comes from someone who herself is young, free and single).

"You just want to have your cake and eat it!" Sweetie said, with more than a hint of irritation in her voice, when I explained to her that I was not yet ready to announce to the world (and every Tom, Dick and Harriet) that we are now an 'item'.

Since Sweetie breezed back into my life, things have been sheer milk and honey between us. That is, until we bumped into Miss XX, an ex of mine.

I introduced Sweetie to Miss XX as, "My f-f-f-f..." Try as hard as I may, I couldn't get the word 'fiancée' to come out, so I simply said, "a friend". That definition seemed to please Miss XX, who patted me in the crutch with a wicked smile and stressed that I must give her a call soon, "for old times' sake."

Sweetie says it was an accident, but moments later her knee and my groin collided and have been colliding ever since, whenever I have difficulty in introducing her properly.

"But Sweetie," I exclaimed, "you know you are my main squeeze."

"Main squeeze? I thought I was your ONLY squeeze?"

Main squeeze, only squeeze, what does it matter? I tried to explain that, for a man, 'main' and 'only' mean the same thing. It's just that it's difficult saying the word 'only'. I might be up for a lifetime commitment, but it doesn't mean I want NO

LONGER AVAILABLE tattoed across my forehead. You see what I'm saying?

But Sweetie wasn't buying that. She reminded me of how I had gone down on one knee and asked her to marry me. Therefore, she concluded, I no longer wanted to be single.

I begged to differ. Technically, yes, I was no longer single. But in reality, being single is a state of mind. And for a lot of guys, it takes years to overcome that psychological divide between bachelor life and being umbilically tied to a woman for life. No matter how much you love her.

But what does that word 'commitment' mean? And why do guys find it so hard to adjust to it mentally?

It's all a question of communication. You say tomato, I say to*may*to... you say potato I say pot*ah*to... Sweetie is happy to tell every man she meets, "Look, there's no point in going down that road because I am already in a relationship," so that they leave her alone. Fair enough. That's her choice. But she insists that I KNOW what 'commitment' REALLY means, but that I just don't want to admit it in public, because it might ruin any chances I have with other women!

That's just not fair to suggest that. Although, I must admit, when you tell a woman who is attracted to you that you're already in a relationship, they act like you've told them you've got the plague. And that often eliminates the possibility of even having that woman as a friend, or a business contact. You see, there are so many innocent reasons why guys don't like to admit to women that they are in a relationship.

Personally, I don't see nothing wrong with carrying on the same bachelor lifestyle I have always led, even though I have made a 'commitment' to Sweetie in private. Ask any single male out there and they'll tell you the same: If being in a relationship didn't affect our lifestyles one bit, most of us would happily call up the pastor, book that wedding day and walk down the aisle tomorrow. At the end of the day we can always take that wedding ring off when we need to. You get me?

Sweetie, I hope you're reading this. Ever since you left me, my life has been miserable. Baby please, please PLEASE come back. And bring my balls with you. I ain't too proud to beg. I can't live without them, I know that now. Let's work it out. I'll do anything you say. In fact, come to think of it, the idea of that tattoo across my forehead is growing on me.

LADIES, YOU KNOW YOU'RE A SLAG IF....

1. *You've slept with Andy Cole and Dwight Yorke at the same time.*

2. *To turn the lights on after sex, you open the car door.*

3. *Having two tampons in at the same time doesn't bother you.*

4. *People say 'Ho, Ho, Ho' when they say you and it's only July.*

5. *Your baby looks familiar, but ike who?*

6. *Changing your sheets comes more than once a day.*

7. *You've got a 'Take a Number' machine outside your bedroom door.*

8. *Your day starts and ends by rolling over.*

9. *Every song reminds you of someone...but who?*

10. *He doesn't even have to buy you a drink.*

11. *The only place you haven't had sex is on the moon.*

12. *Other women begin to call you 'Man's Best Friend'.*

The biggest mistake a man can make, is to come clean about his past to a potential partner. Because women just can't understand how the sum total of a guy's sexual history can read like an ex-girlfriend's telephone number. Guy's are therefore forced to massage the figures to make them look respectable. Or, in other words, to lie, lie and LIE again.

Take Sweetie, for instance. We're back together again but it took almost four weeks of Interfloras, getting down on my knees, grovelling and serenading before she even acknowledged my very existence. Women can be so COLD!

What clinched it for me in the end, was the appeal I made to Sweetie's fellow passengers on the 36B bus route when I followed her home from work one evening recently. As I appealed loudly to their sense of justice and fair play I could see Sweetie feeling SHAME in her seat, but the conductor and passengers (with the exception of two feisty 'man-hating' women on the upper deck) urged her to give me 'one more chance'.

Now, I don't want to blow my own trumpet, but I do know how to make a woman feel sweet, like she's the Queen of Sheba. Remember, I'm an ex-playa. I've had a lot of experience. I practically had Sweetie eating out of my hands when I took her to the poshest restaurant in south London and, who knows, if we had made it through to dessert I might have even convinced her to see things from my point of view — that a man can be in a relationship and STILL be single.

But that was not to be. Half way through the main

course, we were rudely interrupted by Lola, an ex-ex-ex, from years back. The first thing she did was pat me affectionately in the crotch, as if we were still an item, and said, "I hope Mr Johnson's behaving himself and, if not, I hope you've got him well covered."

I should never have gone out with a six foot tall 'Delilah' in the first place. However, at the time (until the spell was broken) Lola was extremely stimulating in an upfront 90's kind of way. But what can I do? Lola will ALWAYS be my ex. And she'll ALWAYS pat me in the crotch when she sees me. That's the way she is, I explained to Sweetie afterwards.

But Sweetie wasn't impressed.

"How come we're always bumping into your ex-girlfriends?"

I explained that it was probably because London's so small.

"So how many more of your exes are we likely to run into?"

"Sweetie baby, how am I supposed to know?"

"Okay, here's one you ought to be able to answer: how many women exactly have you slept with?"

So, that's what this conversation was leading up to. I couldn't help the grin that spread across my face.

You see, it's usually guys who are interested in knowing how many women another guy has slept with. Because guys are so competitive, we always want to know how well we're doing compared to other guys. When a guy asks you that question, you can answer proudly. You can even multiply your total by two or three and you'll get a pat on the back. But when a woman asks you that question, you're in a lose-lose situation. Whatever you say, it's going to either look like you're a whore or that there's something wrong with you. Ladies, men don't like being called slags either, you know. I mean, ladies, what is the point in finding out what you don't want to find out and, what's more, what you can't do anything about?

Sweetie didn't appreciate the grin, but she wasn't going to let it drop until she got an answer. I threw the question back at her (a tactical move I learned from years of infidelity). "How many men have YOU slept with?" I asked, feeling sure that she would be too modest to answer.

"Ten," said Sweetie without hesitation. "You're the eleventh..."

I wasn't expecting that. I wanted to be outraged. Me, number eleven...? But, I had no right to feel upset. Eleven was still a miniscule number in comparison to the sum total of my experience. How was I going to admit to Sweetie that I've been off with eleven women in one week (albeit an exceptional seven days)?! And how on earth was I going to explain to her that a lot of guys I know are surprised by my lack of experience when I tell them that I've only got off with 183 women to date (not counting the two occasions when penetrative sex was unsuccessful). To a woman, 183 might sound a lot, but when you break it down I'm amazed at the restraint to which I have pursued my sexual career.

You see, it's been just over twenty years since I lost my virginity. Broken down, that's about nine women a year. One woman every six weeks. That's hardly anything at all, when you consider that I went out almost every weekend trying to get laid. I practically lived a monk's life. Ask any guy, I'm sure they'll agree. And if they don't, they've probably got something to hide, like I had to hide the truth from Sweetie by any means necessary (remember, this is the mother of my child we're talking about, the woman I'll be umbilically tied to for the rest of my life — *I think*).

So I told her twelve. It didn't sound too bad to me.

"Twelve? Are you sure?" Sweetie asked sceptically.

"Yeah, sure."

"I hope you're not lying to me, D. Because I don't want to have a relationship with someone who lies to me."

I had to lie again, to assure her that I wasn't lying, and that I would not lie to her under any circumstances.

"So, I've only got another two women to meet then..."

"What?!?"

"In our short relationship, I've already met ten women you've slept with. I've only got another two to meet and then no more..."

Shhhhhheeeeeeit! What have I got myself into? London is so small and crawling with exes. How am I going to last two weeks with Sweetie without bumping into a trailerload of them, let alone the rest of my life?

10 BAD EROTIC CHOICES WOMEN MAKE

Ladies, pay attention, I'm not in the habit of giving free consultations, but on this one occasion....

The difference between men and women? That's simple. Women's bodies are just one big erotic erogenous zone, tickle them anywhere with a feather and they start moaning and groaning. Whisper sweet nothings in their ears and their juices start flowing. Sometimes, all you've got to do is light their fire and their knees start quivering.

Men, on the other hand, only have one erotic spot (I'll give you three guesses). Keep that throbbing, ladies, and you'll soon find out where all the good men have gone, because we'll voluntarily walk down the aisle with you, not only vowing to never ever play away from home again, but meaning it, too. Pure and simple. No flim flam, no flaffing around, no beating about the bush (ooops, but you know what I mean).

If you want a good man, ladies, or you've got a good man and want to keep him, or you want to get rid of him for a better man, then stop making these bad erotic choices.

BAD EROTIC CHOICE No. 1

It's not that I'm complaining, but why does erotica have to be such an arduous task? When women are feeling erotic, it might last all night long. Considering that most of us have to work for a living, ladies, why don't you just pretend that you've been erotically satisfied, so that we can go back to sleep? Besides, all this midnight eroticism is so hard on the throat, not to mention the knees, because I keep falling off the flipping trapeze.

GOOD EROTIC CHOICE No 1 — 'The Anvil Stroke'

Bring one hand down, letting it stroke the shaft from the top all the way to the bottom. When it hits the bottom, release it. Meanwhile bring your other hand to the top of the shaft and repeat the stroke, creating an alternating motion.

BAD EROTIC CHOICE No. 2

Eroticism is not about female satisfaction, but about

the full sexual gratification of the male. A woman can still be erotically satisfied without being satisfied (if you see what I mean), but I have yet to have meet a man who is happy unless his meat's beat (if you see what I mean). Besides, it's us fellas who have got the problem with being monogamous, and if we're not happy you're not happy (if you see what I mean).

GOOD EROTIC CHOICE No 2 — 'Climbing the Mountain'
Take the shaft in one hand and gently, sensuously, caress it for about ten seconds, then give it one quick up-and-down stroke. Repeat the sensuous caressing for about ten seconds (perhaps using slow up-and-down strokes), and then give the shaft two quick up-and-down strokes. Repeat the caressing, then give three quick strokes, etc.

BAD EROTIC CHOICE No. 3
Okay, I'm the first to volunteer in a little erotic experimentation. I am not averse to acting out fantasies by dressing up in fancy costumes, having enjoyed playing doctors and nurses as a youngster and subsequently graduating to being the headmaster at a convent school, but I draw my line at having to play the part of the schoolgirl in a gymslip.

GOOD EROTIC CHOICE NO.3 — 'Fire'
Rub the shaft between both palms, as if rubbing two sticks together to create fire. Come on, baby, light my...

BAD EROTIC CHOICE NO. 4
Looking into your man's eyes lovingly while cradling his genitals will only make him feel guilty. If you knew what we were thinking, you would know why we are too ashamed to look into your eyes.

GOOD EROTIC CHOICE NO.4 — 'The Pressure Cock'
With one hand, pull the shaft's skin toward the base. Using the other hand, rhythmically pick various points along the shaft and squeeze gently.

BAD EROTIC CHOICE NO. 5
Slowing down, stopping, or changing your mind just before ejaculation is outta order, distasteful and unbecumming...

GOOD EROTIC CHOICE NO.5 — 'The Hairy Palm Sunday'
Hold the shaft in one hand, with the head sticking up. Using the well-oiled palm of your other hand, slowly and sensitively massage the head. Reverse directions every once in a while.

BAD EROTIC CHOICE NO. 6

Learn to be satisfied, ladies. After men have finally located your 'push button to start' erogenous zones, you don't know what a turn-off it is to discover that we've now got to hit deep and find that G-spot, too, or suffer the consequences.

GOOD EROTIC CHOICE NO.6 — 'The Healing Stroke'

With the shaft resting on the belly, the hand closest to the feet cups the balls. The heel of the palm of the other hand glides up and down the underside of the shaft.

BAD EROTIC CHOICE NO. 7

To a woman, the smallest little thing can be erotic — a cucumber, a carrot etc, and with every sunrise comes a new thing that turns them on. Ladies, there's nothing that turns a man off more than being woken up to run to the all-night supermarket for a bag of fruit and veg.

GOOD EROTIC CHOICE NO.7 — 'The Twist and Shout'

Pull the skin towards the base with one hand. With the other hand, corkscrew the shaft. This can be done with the thumb and first finger or with the whole palm.

BAD EROTIC CHOICE NO. 8

As much as fellas appreciate that female arousal takes longer, why does it have to be so loud and intense when it finally comes? Why does everybody in the same postal code have to know about it? And when I said, "You scratch my back and I'll scratch yours," I didn't mean for you to draw blood.

GOOD EROTIC CHOICE NO.8 — 'The Double Whammy'

Bring both hands down on the shaft. Some are so big they require both hands; if you partner's doesn't, then use the other hand to caress and lightly flutter his balls. If both hands fit along the length of the shaft then move them together, up and down in a pumping motion.

BAD EROTIC CHOICE NO. 9

Declining to invite some of your female friends to an erotic party with your man.

GOOD EROTIC CHOICE NO.9 — 'The Doorknob'

Turn the head like you're trying to open a doorknob coated with grease.

BAD EROTIC CHOICE NO. 10

What's with this multiple orgasm business, ladies? Are you all trying to show off or something? You don't know what a turn-off it is to sit back and twiddle your thumbs while your woman goes off on a marathon orgasm, knowing that she's having a lot more fun than you had.

GOOD EROTIC CHOICE NO.10 — 'The Milker'

Opposite of the Anvil: hands alternate 'milking' the penis, starting at the base and working all the way up.

WAITING TO EXPLODE

No wonder men choose to abandon their baby mothers. Iyanla Vanzant has got a lot to answer for. Thanks to *Acts of Faith*, women believe they can be mother, father, sister, brother, auntie, uncle, godfather, grandfather and great-grandfather all rolled into one.

WHEN WILL THIS MADNESS END?

Like my good friend Patrick 'Baby Father' Augustus says: "If you see a copy of *Acts of Faith* at your baby mother's bedside, pack your bags and find yourself another woman. 'Cause she don't need NO man, NO more.

Take me and Sweetie for instance. Everything was going smoothly. Along with newsreader Moira Stewart, we had attended the recent Sonny Rollins gig at the Barbican. 'Junior' enjoyed the music too, because the moment the beat kicked in he started doing somersaults in Sweetie's ever-expanding womb. Suddenly, Sweetie had a revelation: "We've only got ninety days in which to get married, unless you want our child to grow up with a mother for a father..."

Not wanting to cause a scene in front of Moira, I agreed to marry her when Nigeria win the World Cup. Back in the old days (before Iyanla), that nod would have been as good as a wink to any prospective baby mother. Now though, Sweetie saw the bright red of Moira's name-brand trouser suit and my world exploded in a thousand levels of pain...

She claims she was only trying to help Nigeria win the Cup, and because she doesn't know much about football, she didn't realize that the ball she needed to put in the back of the net was not one of my pair...

As I limped to the car park, Sweetie started speaking in tongues about how the male was a redundant concept. She said that while I've been living in the dark ages, she's been busy being a Woman On The Move (W.O.T.M), meditating daily to come to the realization that she is "the descendant of an unconquered, indomitable people," and that "sometime, somewhere, the blood of a great queen or empress flows through my veins."

Yeah, *right!* I suppose that makes me a great king or an emperor. In which case, Sweetie needs to know (as every chess grandmaster knows) that a queen must support her king always, and without the king there is no queen (WHY DIDN'T YOU PUT THAT IN YOUR BOOK, IYANLA?) I should have told Sweetie so, but there's only so much excruciating pain a guy can take.

N.W.A.'s brilliant rap anthem 'A Bitch Is A Bitch' oozes out of the stereo as we drive home. I am totally overwhelmed by the rap group's lyrical dexterity, exquisitely expressed in rhyme, rhythm and iambic pentameter. The existentialist-phenomenological philosophy in the message of the song had an overall soothing effect on me. However, my enjoyment was cut short as NWA were replaced by a spoken word cassette entitled: 'Daily Reflections To Inspire The Soul':

'It's time for a spring cleaning, time to clear out the

wardrobe of your soul. You will change, but don't be alarmed, it will be for the better. Dust the cobwebs and look into the luggage of your life, see what has passed its 'use by' date, then throw HIM out. The sooner you get rid of him, the sooner you'll be able to carry on with the rest of your life...'

"What the f-?!"

"I don't want you polluting my baby's mind with vulgar rap rubbish," she said stiffly. "The fate of this baby depends on MY love, MY faith and MY achievements."

Hold up. Wait a minute. Rewind. This is MY car. MY stereo. That was one of MY favourite singalongasongs. Besides, the baby's not even born yet.

It was as if Sweetie was reading my thoughts.

"The baby's alive already and being influenced by sounds and the environment all the time. If we don't get married before she's born she'll end up calling Mama 'Pappa'."

Wait a minute. Rewind. Stop that train! *She? Her?!* You mean HE.

Sweetie must be a bloody mind-reader.

"I had a dream that it's a girl," she said.

Do me a favour, Sweetie, stop reading my mind

BLACK HISTORY 12: THE REAL REASON WHY JFK WAS SHOT.

and stop dreaming of girls.

I got home that evening to discover that Sweetie had turned my home into a shrine to Iyanla. Candles flickered everywhere and incense burned. I thought Sweetie had gone to fetch me my bottle of rum to get over the shock, instead she had disappeared to that 'temple within' to pour out a libation to the 'goddesses of the universe'.

WAIT JUST ONE MINUTE NOW!

Am I not the master in my own home? Am I wrong to say romantic things to Sweetie such as, "We'll get married if you can can guess the next tune that the deejay plays on the radio." Am I wrong to expect total obedience and subservience from the woman who's carrying my son and heir?

ANSWER ME THAT, IYANLA VANZANT, OR ANY OTHER WOMAN WHO DARES TO TAKE UP THE CHALLENGE.

SWINGING BLACK BRITAIN

I'd be the first to admit that I ain't the most religious of people but the pastor was certainly one of the most entertaining speakers I'd heard in a long time. He was on a roll and it was great to see the enthusiasm in which he blasted the 'growing sexual permissiveness' in society.

He kept going on about wife swapping and swinging couples to the point where I thought that this guy must have some sort of distorted view of what is going on out there. Maybe he's seen too many swinging sixties films, I reasoned. I don't know of any of that shit going down so it can't be happening, right?

Maybe pastor knows more about such matters than I do. I picked up a copy of the free ad newspaper 'Loot', last week for a motor and happened to glance in the personal section *(as you do when you're looking to buy a car)* . I was absolutely shocked at the sheer weight of ads from couples who wanted to connect, literally, with other couples. I'm telling you, pages and pages of the same shit. Last time I looked in Loot to buy a car I'm sure there was only a handful of similar ads.

I was chatting to an ex a few days ago about the issue and naively saying that "this couple swinging business is something that bored bank managers in Surbiton get up to and black couples definitely ain't into that thing."

According to her I am out of touch with what's going on out there. Among the interesting tales she had to tell was that of her sister and partner who are involved in a private black 'club' with about 200 'members'. This club has many wealthy Africans among its ranks and parties are regularly held in very expensive private addresses where they swap partners. New members can only join if recommended by another member. The more she told me about the occupations of the members the more it dawned on me that I must know some of these people but obviously don't have a clue what they get up to in their spare time.

She also told me of a circle of about a dozen black couples in south London who have a 'party scene' going down on a regular basis. Apparently some of the set also meets up in a well-known West End nightclub to connect with similarly minded white professional couples. She had so many stories of swinging couples (including one involving a well-known black footballer) that I started to wonder if I'm Mr Prude or something and the rest of you lot have a different idea of what constitutes a good time.

Personally I have absolutely no desire to join swinging black Britain. I think that couples who have to get their thrills by getting it off with others couples have lost the plot big time. If you can't have a good time with your partner then there ain't gonna be much of a future for the two of you. If you have to bring in outside activity to make it happen then, bwoy, things have reached the point of staleness.

I can't see how a relationship will last in the long term once folk embark on this kind of t'ing. I don't care how right-on or sexually liberated a guy thinks he is. Deep down in his sub-conscious he ain't going to think too much of his woman after he sees her being flexed by some other geezer. Likewise most women won't feel too good seeing their man getting off with another female.

Nah man. The pastor was definitely right on this one. Wife swapping and that kind of shit is something that is best left to sad, kinky, white, middle-class civil servants in suburbia who lack the imagination to make their own sex life any more exciting than a wet afternoon in Bradford.

Reluctantly, I have come to accept the indisputable fact that women are smarter than guys and, yes, if you force my hand, superior to us.

This is due to the fact that the female brain has a larger density of grey matter than the male brain. Faced with the overwhelming scientific evidence, I throw up both my hands and say, "Women, you run (certain) t'ings..."

Take Sweetie, for example, she's much better than me at ironing. Every time I iron, I burn a hole in one of her favourite dresses, but she still hasn't learned.

Cooking also. Thanks to all those extra grey cells, Sweetie cooked me a wicked meal last night which was washed down by a tasty glass of Guinness punch which she blended together just right. It was absolutely *boonoonoonoos*. Me, on the other hand, can not fry an egg. Honest, ladies. The one time I felt obliged to surprise Sweetie with breakfast in bed, the toast caught fire, it burned down the kitchen and set alight the dishwasher, and now Sweetie's got to wash the dishes by hand.

On account of all those extra brain cells, she washes dishes excellently. I mean, the last time I squeezed out half a bottle of Fairy Liquid, Sweetie's most precious crystal glasses slipped out of my hands accidently, one by one, and smashed into a thousand pieces on the floor. I had given her prior warning that men are unable to do washing up because of the lack of grey cells in the male brain, but she didn't believe me. Oh well...

Sweetie's much better at cleaning up the house as

well, and after she had carefully dusted up each broken piece of glass, I bought her some superglue to put it all back together again. You see, she's much better at solving jigsaw puzzles than I am.

With the baby only four weeks away, Sweetie's suggesting that I terminate that long-time tradition of having the boyz and Pastor Blunt around at my place for a marathon Friday night/Saturday morning domino session in the living room, where we kick back after a long week of hard work, with a couple of crates of brew.

Terminate? What kind of language is that for my baby to be hearing in his mother's womb? A word like that will scare the hell out of him.

"If you're talking about *our* baby," Sweetie began, "*she* is more concerned with the fact that her father still hasn't put up the shelves that are needed to create extra space for *her* arrival, and *she* is wondering when you'll finally get round to going to an ante-natal class."

It is a biological, mathematical, genealogical impossibility that my baby's going to turn out to be anything but a fully paid-up member of Guys Inc. Girls just don't occur in our family. Not unless the mother has cut off a chicken's head under a full moon and danced naked around a steaming cauldron anti-clockwise. You see, obeah's another thing that women are better at. How else is Sweetie going to be able to give birth? It is physically, mathematically and logically impossible for a camel to pass through the eye of a needle, likewise for a baby the size of a regulation basketball to pass through a woman's vagina. As I explained to Sweetie, in my many years of researching women's vaginas ("for purely anthropological reasons, you understand") I have yet to feel one with the width to push a basketball in. Now, if a basketball can't go in, how the bumboclaat is one supposed to come out without a touch of obeah?

Sweetie doesn't like to hear that. Whenever I show her that level of reasoning, a look of pain clouds her face and she groans as if to say, 'Fair cop, men are much smarter than women. Hubble bubble toil and trouble, I am also a fully paid-up member of Obeah Inc.' Instead, she said she'd like to shove a basketball up my behind so that I can share in the child-bearing experience.

"Anyway," Sweetie continued, "whether the baby turns out to be a boy or a girl has less to do with obeah and more to do with YOU: the male carries the determining factor — the x and the y chromosomes..."

Say what you want, Sweetie. All I know is, that spermatozoa left me in perfectly good male condition. Next month we'll all know whether you're an obeah woman or not. If it's a girl, I'm going to go looking for an exorcist for your ass, Sweetie, I swear to God I am.

SURPRISE!

What I and a lot of other brothas can't understand, is why it is that nearly every black woman you meet nowadays has made the life-shattering mistake of becoming yet another statistic in the continuing adventures of a serial baby father. Why can't ladies recognize a wotless, good-for-nothing layabout when he comes bearing flowers, chocolates and a cheesy smile? Why don't you demand that he uses a condom when he succeeds in sweet-talking you into bed, or at least make sure that you have his credit card number just in case he disappears the moment the Predictor turns out positive?

Not so long ago, when men were bold and inside toilets had not been invented, a brotha could reasonably expect to be marrying a lilywhite/chocolatedrop virgin even if he himself had dipped his wick in every conceivable orifice he could find. Nowadays, though, it's so hard to find a sista who is ready for marriage and isn't carrying excess baggage from a previous relationship. It's a sign of the times, I guess. Britain has the highest number of teenage pregnancies in Western Europe and, unfortunately, a lot of those happen to be black mothers.

You see, back when we were all teenagers sistas only had eyes for the cool, handsome, slick arseholes of this world, while guys like myself were considered 'boring' because we were more concerned with passing our exams and getting into university than trying to stick a bush. Now, years later, when so many of those same women are lumbered with that cool, handsome, slick bad bwoy's pickney, guys like myself are suddenly considered 'reliable', 'a safe pair of hands'.

These very same women expect to meet a 'reliable' man gullible enough to willingly take on the burden of another man's child. As if we're blind as well as stupid. "Love me, love my baby," they insist.

No, ladies, that can't work. Why should your new man be prepared to clean up someone else's mess when society at large has had enough? Just the other day the government decided that it will lock up all those absent baby fathers who are trying to shirk their responsibilities, and I say "good", because if they're not prepared to be a father to their children, the rest of us aren't, either.

Yet still, these very same women expect their new man to understand that they and their child are umbilically linked and that the man's not just getting a lover out of the relationship, but a son or daughter, too. No man is happy with that .

I, therefore, must be out of my mind. I was the last person who thought that I was going to end up being a substitute pappa for somebody else's rude pickney. When I'm in a relationship, I like to know that it's "me" and "you" or "you" and "me", not "you, me and your old man's baby." Let's face it, no woman can serve two masters...

Sweetie waited until I was just past the point of no return before she even mentioned that little bundle of joy called 'Brat'. Only Brat's not so little any more and he can't take the fact that anybody other than his pappa is sleeping with his mother.

Sweetie says I'm paranoid, that a three-year-old wouldn't accidently on purpose headbutt me in the

goolies and that it's just a coincidence that his favourite record happens to be Cat Stevens' 'I'm Gonna Get Me A Gun', which he turns up at full volume every time I step in the room. But I know for a fact that someone in this house poured salt in my lager, put itching powder in my underpants and cat's hair in my Ventolin asthma inhaler.

It just goes to show how little mothers know about their own children, especially boy children. Brat, who insists on calling me 'coconut head' when we're alone, has informed me in no uncertain terms that I am not his daddy, and I never will be.

Can you blame me for giving him a good, hard whack on his neckback to teach him that there's only room for one don in this household? Little did I know that his wotless father's number was logged on the telephone memory and that Brat knew which button was a direct hotline to 'the CSA's Most Wanted'.

Next thing I know, a King-Kong lookalike walks in with rippling muscles that could only have been developed from spending all day every day in the gym. With his knee on the bridge of my nose, while Brat frantically waved his thumbs down, he lets me know that just because I happen to be sexing his woman, it is not my job to discipline his youth.

"Love me, love my baby," Sweetie insisted when I told her that her son needed a government health warning tattooed across his forehead. That's another thing about women, when you tell them that their children are unruly, undisciplined, badly brought up and rude, they take it personally.

Brat is not my problem. Now that decision time has come, Miss Tee has to choose between a loving, happy, fulfilled and full of sex life with me, and a thousand lonely nights with Brat. It's him or me. She needs to remember that she can always have another kid, but she probably won't ever find another man that can light her fire like I can.

The Great Big Lie about black men is that we are irresponsible fathers who abandon our pickney willy nilly (yes, I know, that phrase again, but under the circumstances...) making scant if any provisions for their moral, social and spiritual needs, not to talk of ducking, diving and juggling just to stay one step ahead of the Child Support Agency.

If this insufferable Great Big Lie were being perpetrated by the white man, it would make us wanna holler and throw up our arms crying 'racism'. So how come women can, without let or hindrance, chat the Great Big Lie nearly every day in the hairdressing salons that plague our communities up and down the country?

I know for a fact that there isn't a guy out there who could even contemplate giving up the fruit of his loins, the flesh of his flesh, the blood of his ancestors without the mother of all battles or, at the very least, a most unreasonable baby mother. I know for another fact, that the guy ain't been built who is so callous, cold, dark, so evil as to refuse to do everything in his power to protect and provide for his seed — figuratively speaking, and otherwise.

Take me for instance. At 10.00am last Thursday, that little devil in my left ear was advising me to change my name and "Get on that flight to Rio. It's your last chance!"

At 10.03 I was bundled into the delivery room by a midwife who claimed that my presence was required. Inside, Sweetie was wrestling with that mathematical conundrum of how to force a regulation-size basketball down a hole the diameter of a ping-pong ball. It was agonizing to watch. Fortunately, I will never know how agonizing it was to attempt.

So I did my bit, I sang:

"Push, Sweetie, push

An' mek the yout' come out..."

Sweetie was clearly delirious. She whacked me with a well-delivered roundhouse kick to the face, followed by a left, and a right uppercut, all the time screaming with unprintable verbosity.

"It's all perfectly normal," the midwife assured me, adding that a foot in your birthing partner's face makes the baby go down easier, aiding delivery.

At 10.17 precisely, the little devil in my ear offered me one last and final chance to do a disappearing act. "Okay," the devil said, "I'll make a deal with you, if it's a boy, hey, stick around. But if it's a girl — Copacabana here we come!"

At 10.19 a tiny head popped out from between Sweetie's legs, followed by a pair of arms and legs.

At 10.20 I was on my knees, sobbing uncontrollably and thanking the Lord of Lords, the King of Kings, the Conquering Lion of the tribe of Judah and anyone else I could think of for my wrinkled bundle of joy. I was instantly madly, truly, deeply in love. Ain't nothing more beautiful than a new-born baby. Especially when he looks like you. Show me a guy who could turn his back on that to walk out of the door and just keep walking, and I'll show you a living duppie.

But, of course, there ain't no such thing, it's just one Great Big Lie.

What I'm basically saying, ladies, is I now know that the REAL MAN ain't been made who is cold enough to abandon his own flesh, skin and bones to the mercy of the lottery of life and a bitter, possibly twisted, baby mother. Therefore, unless you've been consorting and conceiving with a vampire, I can only deduce that the father of your child does everything in his power to provide and protect for the little nipper. The only other option is that you left him with no choice but to leave.

Ask yourself, ladies, are you all going to desist in cavorting with vampires?

Meanwhile, back at the labour ward, I inform Sweetie that I am now the proud father of a handsome baby son. "I told you it was going to be a boy, didn't I," I say beaming. "Yes, a beautiful baby boy, the only thing is, I can't seem to find his willy anywhere..."

END... *FOR NOW.*